———————◆———————

Very special thank you
to my great friend and
talented writer
Leo Adam Biga
for helping me
write this book and
make it a reality.

———————◆———————

CROSSING BRIDGES

A Priest's Uplifting Life Among the Downtrodden

Father Ken Vavrina

Omaha, Nebraska

All photos are from the author's personal collection and remain his sole property. Cover photo: Father Vavrina met with Mother Teresa in 1990 at the center for Mentally Handicapped in Calcutta, which was funded by the Kennedy family. He said Mother Teresa typically put her hand to her chin when she was thinking about something serious.

Uplifting Publishing books are available from your favorite bookseller or from www.upliftingpublishing.com

Uplifting Publishing
c/o CMI
13518 L. Street
Omaha, NE 68137

ISBN: 978-1-936840-86-1 (ppk)
ISBN: 978-1-936840-87-8 (Mobi)
ISBN: 978-1-936840-88-5 (EPUB)

Library of Congress Cataloging Number on file with the publisher.

Printed in the USA

10 9 8 7 6 5 4 3 2

To the people in need that were so
much a part of my life.

Contents

Introduction: Crossing Bridges 1

1   "Thank God you're here." 7

2   Raised Up: Coming of Age in Nebraska 15

3   Seminary: I Gave It a Shot 25

4   Winnebago-Macy: On the Reservation 29

5   Omaha: Racial Tension, Civil Rights 35

6   Wounded Knee: "Father, we need medicine." 51

7   South Sioux City: Longing to Become
     Unimportant Doing Christ's Work 61

8   Yemen: The Leper Village Known
     as the City of Light 67

9   Yemen: Learning the Joy of Service to
     Society's Outcasts 73

10   Yemen: I Just Got Out of Jail 99

11   India: With Mother Teresa 117

12   India: "God only sees the love in our hearts." 135

13   Liberia: Civil War, Warlords, and Lawlessness........... 153

14   The Journey Home via Cuba 181

15   Not Finished Yet.. 197

16   Final Crossing.. 203

INTRODUCTION

———————◆———————

Crossing Bridges

I never intended to write this memoir.

People long ago began encouraging me to commit my life to paper. I heard a lot of, "Father Ken, you should write a book." I suppose they felt my unusual experiences could offer some inspiration or enlightenment to readers.

For most of my adult years, I have been a Roman Catholic priest. I was ordained in 1962. More than a third of my fifty-plus years as a priest were spent in foreign lands. My travels brought me in close contact with the famous, most notably Mother Teresa, now well on her way to sainthood, and with the infamous, namely the deposed Liberian dictator Charles Taylor, now imprisoned after being convicted of war crimes.

Born in Bruno and raised in Clarkson, Nebraska, I come from a family that was not particularly religious. The thought of joining the clergy never occurred to me through most of my teens, though the prospect of traveling abroad most certainly did cross my mind from the time I was a small boy. But the priesthood? Not a chance.

In fact, a girl and I seriously dated through high school, and we had an understanding that one day we would get married. That was the plan, until one day…ah, but that is getting ahead of the story.

Before I go back, I must fast-forward for just a moment because it is important for you to know the reason why I finally decided to write my memoir. You see, as I neared eighty years of age, I realized my life has been all about crossing bridges. Those bridges have been geographic and cultural.

Crossing has meant making commitments to new ways of living and to new groups of people. It has meant responding to dire human needs. Each time I made the leap, I came to a deeper appreciation for the sanctity of life and for the importance of relieving suffering in the world. Each crossing has enriched my life in significant ways.

I have had the privilege of serving people in five countries on four continents. In the United States, I ministered to Native Americans, African-Americans, and Hispanics during the height of the civil rights movement. Those were heady times. Then, in the course of nineteen years of missionary work overseas, I comforted lepers in the Arab nation of Yemen. I oversaw relief efforts for victims of an earthquake in southern Italy. I supervised aid to and regenerated the agricultural sector for the poorest of the poor in India, Bangladesh, and Nepal. I secured food and medicine for war refugees in the African nation of Liberia. There was also a controversial medical supply mission I led to Cuba.

In my own country, I saw firsthand the devastation that alcohol and capricious US government policy has had on Native Americans. I went to Wounded Knee to deliver medical supplies during the 1973 standoff.

I witnessed African-American anger in response to police misconduct. I was on the streets in North Omaha when a 1969 riot erupted after a trigger-happy police officer who shot and killed an unarmed girl, was let off scot-free by a judge. Fires set that night in anger over the court's decision torched North 24th Street, whose once-thriving business district has yet to recover almost a half century later. I have been in the homes of Mexican immigrants who braved life, limb, and liberty to come here illegally in order to give their families better lives.

At the request of Mother Teresa, who became a very dear friend, I cleaned and comforted lepers in Yemen for five years. I was jailed there for ten days before being expelled from the country. I cradled the dead and dying in the slums of Calcutta, where I directed a Catholic Relief Services mission that assisted millions.

Catholic Relief Services later sent me to the middle of a civil war in Liberia, where I struck deals with tyrant Charles Taylor to get medical supplies and food to sick and starving people at the mercy of warlords. A supply ship I leased to bring in critical medicines and foodstuffs suffered damage coming into port. As it took on water, armed rebels approached, forcing the captain, crew, and me to abandon the ship and its supplies to the spoils of war.

Yes. An interesting life.

None of this may have happened, though, were it not for a childhood incident. When I was about nine years old, my family and I went by automobile on vacation to California and were returning by way of Texas at night. We were in El Paso, near the bridge that crosses the border into Mexico, and I remember my mom telling me, "On the other side of that bridge is Mexico," and right then and there I vowed to myself, *One day I'm going to cross that bridge.* This is so indelibly marked in my mind that it might as well have happened yesterday.

Many years later, I did go to Mexico, not by way of that same bridge from my childhood, but I crossed over nonetheless. I firmly believe that pledge I made as a boy prepared me to embrace and seek out new horizons. It informed my willingness to serve Native Americans at the Winnebago Reservation in Nebraska, Hispanics in South Sioux City, African-Americans in northeast Omaha, and all the different nationalities and ethnicities I encountered abroad.

But some other events happened that also motivated me to work overseas. I got caught up in the fervor of the civil rights movement. The spirit of those times put me in a frame of mind to be a social justice advocate willing to go wherever I could to serve the destitute and the oppressed.

In the 1970s, I was pastoring churches in Omaha's inner city when I read about how the cardinal and archbishop of Montreal, Canada, Paul-Émile Léger, upon reaching retirement age, announced he was going to work with lepers in Cameroon, Africa. More than anything else, it triggered in me a desire to go overseas. That realization is particularly important to my story.

Léger's example really had an effect on me. This was just around the time I saw Mother Teresa speak at Boys Town, where in 1976 she was honored with the Father Flanagan Award for Service to Youth for the work she and her Missionaries of Charity did with families in India. It was also around the time I read her biography *Something Beautiful for God*. Her story made an indelible impression on me.

Léger's decision to serve lepers posed a challenge to the rest of us clergy. Here he was, an old man who had risen to the exalted position of cardinal archbishop in the church. He was on top of the world. But he was going to leave all that behind to work with lepers. He could have had a comfortable life in Canada, but to elect to go to Cameroon to have a difficult life and to undergo hardships—well, that really blew me away.

So I answered the call to follow his lead, and those nineteen years I spent abroad were the most rewarding of my life.

But it was not until recently, when reflecting upon my life, that I understood just what an impact his and Mother Teresa's examples made on me. I saw with perfect clarity how there was this direct connection between my desire to cross that bridge in Mexico and my eventually crossing all those literal and figurative bridges. I was not only heeding my natural curiosity to find out what was on the other side, but also living out Christ's good shepherd path among the poor and the forgotten.

As soon as I made that connection, I told myself I was going to write a book. This is that book. My hope is that my story will do some good by inspiring others to take their own leap of faith and go on a service journey or mission of their own. It need not be halfway around the world either. There are plenty of folks in need of help right in our own communities, right in our own backyards.

In a temporal sense, I do not have many more bridges to cross. My final crossing, whenever that should come, will be in the hereafter, where, I believe, as the saying goes, I will meet my maker. If I am asked in heaven to give an accounting of myself, it would be that whenever called to serve my fellow man, I answered—no matter how distant or unfamiliar or harsh or even dangerous the environment. I do not mean to pat myself on the back. Rather, I have always believed in doing God's work to benefit my brothers and sisters because I know they would help me if they could.

The message I wish to convey in this book is that if I could do this work, you can too. I am an average person. I come from humble beginnings that taught me it is your actions that count, not the things you accumulate. Thus, I have tried to live my life by making do with what little material possessions I have and by doing good for others.

There is nothing remarkable about me in this regard, yet I have been blessed to lead a most fulfilling life following this ethos of simplicity. It has been a core part of my experience wherever I have lived. The nature of my work has taken me to some fascinating places around the world and introduced me to the full spectrum of humanity, good and bad.

Stripping away the encumbrances of things and titles is truly liberating because then it is just you and the person beside you or in front of you. There is nothing more to hide behind. That is when two human hearts truly connect.

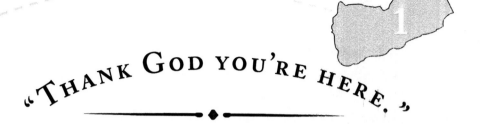

"Thank God you're here."

M other Teresa was a tiny, gentle woman, yet she exerted a powerful presence. She had a gravity and a charisma and an intensity about her that you could not ignore. She was one of those people who changed the energy in whatever space she occupied and in whoever's company she joined.

She was direct and strong and to the point. There was a fierceness and determination as well as a mischievousness to her that I would get to know well. She even laughed at my jokes.

I had arrived in Rome to find Mother Teresa and to ask how I could serve. Her organization, the Missionaries of Charity, run by this tiny dynamo known worldwide, was based out of Calcutta with an office in Rome.

It was 1977. And I, a humble parish priest from Nebraska who had served Native Americans on their reservation and black Americans in volatile crime-ridden neighborhoods during the civil rights struggles, yearned now to serve overseas.

Little did I realize I would soon be in a country I couldn't find on a map, scraping rotting, dead skin off lepers until I was arrested for being a suspected CIA agent and forced to lie in my own diarrhea-caused stench in a Yemeni prison.

But my travels leading up to decades of service to the poorest of the poor began in Rome. It is customary for visiting priests to say Mass at Mother Teresa's Mother House in Rome, and that is what I did. Mother Teresa visited me after Mass as I was eating breakfast. I expressed my desire to serve.

Throwing her hands up in the air—she always threw her hands up in the air—she said in perfect English, "Oh, Father, thank God you're here. We need a priest in Yemen to work with our sisters in the leper village. Would you be willing to go to Yemen to work alongside our sisters with the lepers?"

I simply replied, "Sure."

The reason I jumped at the request without hesitation is that this is precisely what I left the United States to do. I was prepared to accept any opportunity to be of service, even if it meant working with lepers. And Yemen? I had no idea where it was.

She explained that the priest who had been at the leper colony in Yemen had contracted hepatitis and had to be medically evacuated out of the country. That same day, Mother Teresa accompanied me to the Yemeni embassy in Rome. I obtained my visa and all the other documents and clearances I needed to travel. With my own money, I purchased a one-way ticket to an adventure I have never forgotten.

By evening I was aboard a plane on my way to an Arabic land in Western Asia that I knew nothing about. I remember as the plane was descending into Yemen, the pilot came over the intercom to announce the local time. He sarcastically commented about the extreme time difference, really a time warp, when he said, "Be sure to set your watches back three hundred years."

After a five-hour drive by Peugeot station wagon, I had indeed traveled back in time and space to a leper colony. My only belongings were packed in a small suitcase.

The sisters of the Missionaries of Charity lived in a convent in what Mother Teresa called the City of Light. I was shown to a small hut that was to become my home for the next five years. I slept on a mat on the dirt floor. There are no tables or chairs for eating, so I sat cross-legged—often difficult for me with my long legs—on the hard floor for my meals, which I would prepare each day from fresh ingredients I would purchase at the nearby open-air market. With no refrigeration, I had to buy what I would eat immediately, and my meal was often a simple local mix of grain and vegetables cooked over a propane-fueled hot plate.

The shades covering the window openings were for privacy and nothing more. The first time I rolled up a shade, a snake greeted me, sunning himself on the open-air window ledge.

No running water. No electricity. I knew my task was to acclimate myself to a culture and a people I had never before experienced. But nothing had prepared me for the horrors of leprosy.

Leprosy. A disease we Americans had only heard about—and often reacted to with horror and disgust. And ignorance.

The first day I visited the leper village, I began exploring the huts packed with cots, upon which lay humans suffering the ravages of leprosy—some with open, oozing sores. I surveyed the misery, hands firmly planted in my front pants pockets all day. I was afraid I too would contract leprosy.

And the smell. The smell was the rotting flesh of villagers who had fled their homes to avoid the shame on their families. They sought solace with us, and had lost fingers, hands, feet, noses, and their very lives. They died not from leprosy, but from tuberculosis or other infections that thrived among those too weak to fight common diseases.

Eventually, I removed my hands from my pockets. I was there to serve the lepers.

I watched the sisters—four trained registered nurses—tend to the dying and followed their lead. We would don rubber gloves supplied by the German Catholic organization that shipped in medical supplies and medicine—another of Mother Teresa's many negotiations.

Using a surgical instrument that looked much like a sharpened razor-blade box cutter, I would sit in a chair opposite a patient who was also sitting in a chair at his bedside (most of our patients were men) as he presented me a diseased foot or arm or nose and scrape the dead skin onto a cloth. We would later bury the infected materials or burn them.

If a patient was too weak to sit, I would kneel on the dirt floor at the bedside and perform the scraping. Mercifully, leprosy causes nerve damage, so the daily scraping process itself was not painful. In fact, I later watched as local Yemeni doctors would amputate legs, hands, and arms without using anesthesia.

My first patient was a relatively young man, perhaps thirty years old, although no one in Yemen lived to what we consider old age. He presented me with his hands, one by one, and I learned quickly how to serve. I came to love these people. They became my community, and we theirs.

I checked the inside crook of my arms daily for telltale white spots on that tender skin that might signal the start of leprosy, which, if caught at this early stage, was highly curable. I always checked. Leprosy is transmitted by blood, and I was certainly vulnerable despite our precautions.

The first time Mother Teresa visited the City of Light while I was there, we were preparing to expand the overburdened medical facilities. We had so many amputations, we simply needed more room for patients, and we had made arrangements with the Ministry of Health to expand the hospital.

But Mother said no. No, the first thing we were going to build is a mosque, she said, so people can pray to their God. Although we were forbidden by the Yemeni government to proselytize our Catholic teachings, we respected the Muslim faith among the lepers.

My daily life was simple in the City of Light. I breakfasted at the convent after I said Mass for the sisters. My mornings were spent teaching English at a private school, and then a fellow on a motorcycle would pick me up and take me to the City of Light where I would work with the lepers until evening. The sisters would drive me to the souq (an open-air market) where I would buy whatever I was making for my meal, and I would sit on a mat on my dirt floor and prepare my modest meal of vegetables and local sorghum.

Until one day, five years into my service in Yemen, a government security officer asked me to present my documents at their offices. I was grilled for two hours and put on house arrest at the leper colony.

The sisters in the convent's chapel in Taiz, Yemen. Part of Mother Teresa's
Missionaries of Charity, they were also nurses who lovingly tended the
medical needs of the lepers.

It seemed that Peace Corps workers were getting a little
too close to the war between North and South Yemen (the
communists were in the south; I was working in the north),
and the young Americans were taking photos of planes at the
border. The government went crazy and was sure I was working
with them and for the CIA.

About two months later, I was ordered to go to the capital
of Sana'a to defend myself. I communicated via fax with the
American Embassy in Yemen. At that point the ambassador
knew I was going to jail.

I was locked inside a room in a building, it wasn't a jail,
but it might as well have been. About fifty of us men were so

crowded inside the windowless room—so tightly packed we couldn't all lie down at the same time. We took turns.

I was the only Westerner. I was resigned to the fact that I would be locked up and assumed it might be for at least six months while the American Embassy sorted things out. The others were thought to be war sympathizers.

At least they were locals and acclimated to the polluted water they served us to drink. Even in the winter, our daily temperatures reached a dry 85. Unfortunately for us all, the water gave me diarrhea, and I wasn't able to wait for our once-a-day exercise in the courtyard to relieve myself there.

I stunk up the jail, covered in my own feces. I could hear gunshots and people screaming at night.

I would still be in Yemen today if they hadn't eventually thrown me out of the country.

RAISED UP:

———————•◆•———————

Coming of Age in Nebraska

I was born January 1, 1935, in Bruno. The tiny northeast Nebraska town was founded by émigrés from Bruno, Czechoslovakia. Just like Clarkson, the nearby Czech town I grew up in, Bruno is located amid a rolling landscape that residents affectionately call the Bohemian Alps.

My mother's mother, Mary, came from the old country as a sixteen-year-old girl. I admire her courage because she came on a ship all by herself, and she did not know a word of English. She had a job waiting for her in Cleveland, Ohio, with a Presbyterian minister and his wife.

Somebody put her on a train in New York to Cleveland, where she worked for almost a year. Then she heard there was a Czech settlement in Omaha, Nebraska. So she came to the Midwest and worked as an upstairs maid in the Prague Hotel next door to the Bohemian Cafe. She did not know a soul in

Omaha. The bartender at the hotel was a man by the name of Frank Slama, who was a young émigré himself. They soon started a romance and eventually married.

My paternal grandfather emigrated from Vienna, Austria. He brought with him his prized possession—a violin. He was a Bohemian who spoke German. He settled in Omaha before moving to Clarkson and its growing Czech community. He established several businesses in Clarkson, including a hotel.

I marvel at how enterprising this man was. With no money at all, he built a beautiful bar and hotel. The downstairs was a saloon, and the upstairs a hotel, and that is where the family lived at the beginning. He became a very successful businessman. The building is still there in town and looks like a million bucks. My grandfather was evidently quite a man, but I never knew him because he died when I was just a baby.

However, I was close to my maternal grandma, Mary Slama. She was as sweet as sugar. She died when I was in high school.

Back in the day, there was a ranch north of Clarkson, and the cowboys would come into town on horseback. They would bring their horses right into the bar. By the time I came along, the cowboys had disappeared, and I worked at the bar making hamburgers for the locals.

My mother was born Marie Slama. She was named after her mother. She grew up in Clarkson and then went to what was then called Wayne State Teachers College. She worked in Abie, a town next to Bruno, where she was teaching school when she met my father. My mom had a brother, Frank, and two sisters, Libby and Pina. Aunt Pina's husband had the printing press in Clarkson.

My father, Edward Vavrina, was from Bruno. He grew up on a farm between Bruno and Abie. When I was a child, he was a barber transitioning into the insurance business. He had a barber shop right on main street in Bruno. My older brother, Ron, was born four years before me, in 1931. We lived in Bruno at the start.

When Ron was nine and I was four, our father died. One day he was coming home from work. The town was having a harvest festival, and a man on a ladder was struggling to reach an outdoor light that needed changing. He was too short for the job so my dad, who was tall, said, "C'mon down, I can do it."

And my dad went up the ladder. He accidentally brushed up against a live wire, and the shock he received knocked him down to the ground, where he hit his head on the concrete curb. Bystanders took him to the hospital in David City. The doctor who examined him told him he was fine. He came home. But within hours, he developed a blood clot and was rushed to St. Joseph Hospital in Omaha, about sixty miles away. He died on the operating table.

After Dad died, my mother and brother and I moved to Clarkson to live with my grandma Mary and my aunt Libby and her husband, Joe Vacin, who owned a big auto and implement business. Clarkson was a very good business town. It still is today. We all lived in a big house right in town.

With our father gone, Uncle Joe became a father figure to Ron and me. Uncle Joe and Aunt Libby had no children of their own, so we became their surrogate kids. Ron and I just assumed we were both going to go into the family's implement business one day. Ron did but God had other plans for me.

Oh, I did work in the garage sweeping floors. I got promoted to work in the parts department. When I was a little older, I changed tires and washed cars. I was a flunky.

Uncle Joe started Vacin, Inc., back in 1922. It was both a hardware and automotive business then. He later added a John Deere implement line. My brother, Ron, joined the business after graduating from high school. They expanded the implement side into the neighboring town of Dodge for a time. Ron eventually took over the company and developed a construction department building air-tight, sealed grain storage silos. He later added a center pivot irrigation sales and service department.

His son and my nephew, Randy, joined the business and was appointed to manage the construction and irrigation divisions. Randy's brother Gary also joined the business. Eventually the implement-automotive division and the construction-irrigation division became separate businesses that go by the names Vacin, Inc., and Vavrina, Inc., respectively. I am proud of my family's entrepreneurial legacy and the fact that companies with the names Vacin and Vavrina remain two of the largest employers in Colfax County.

When I was a kid, my mom finished her bachelor's degree and went on to earn a master's degree. She taught elementary school in Clarkson for thirty-eight years. I attended public school, but I never had her as a classroom teacher. She was well liked and admired. When I think of my mom today, I think of her with a pink dress on sitting in the kitchen by the phone. She was smart as a whip and just as sweet as sugar. She supported me and my brother. I knew everything she wanted me to do. I didn't always do it.

I really had two moms. There was Mother, and then there was Aunt Libby. Where my mother was more quiet and gentle, rarely raising her voice, Libby was more earthy. However, in all the years we lived together under the same roof, I never heard them argue once. It was just a really good, loving family environment.

Uncle Joe would take me hunting. I shot my first jackrabbit with him. The first time he took me hunting, it was a Thanksgiving, and I was playing touch football with my friends. Joe said, "C'mon, I'm going out to the farm, maybe we'll see some rabbits."

He had a nearby spread chock full of small game. It was a beautiful day, and so it did not take much convincing for me to break away from the game to run inside the house to grab my .410 shotgun. So off we went.

We were no sooner out in the field when we came up on this big jackrabbit just sitting there. I lifted the barrel to aim and shoot, but I missed with my first shot. With the rabbit still in my sights, I shot again and hit. I have a picture of me with the jackrabbit. I used to go hunting a lot by myself with my dog Chips.

During the Second World War everything was rationed—tires, gasoline, butter. As an extended family trying to stretch things, we shared expenses. We did things together too. For instance, we would go on family trips. My uncle Joe loved to fish. We would sometimes trek to Minnesota, the Land of Ten Thousand Lakes, to take advantage of its well-stocked waters. Eagle Lake in extreme southern Minnesota was one of our favorite spots. I never saw so much water.

We usually stayed in a cabin. I saw bear and deer and owls. It was a wonderful experience. I loved it. My uncle had an outboard motor, and he would rent a boat and off we would go onto the lake. My mom and my aunt were terrible fisherwomen. They were always snagging, and Uncle Joe didn't have a chance to fish at all because he was either unsnapping their lines or baiting their hooks. But we still had fun.

I have pictures of myself with a sailor cap on standing in front of the Welcome to Minnesota sign. That was a big deal. We even went into Canada to fish. I remember once, on our way to Minnesota, we drove through the Winnebago, Nebraska, reservation. My eyes were as big as saucers because there was a Native American woman with a papoose on her back. It was my first time seeing Native Americans in person. I could not have known then that I would live and work among the Winnebago.

When I got older, our family went on trips every summer. Part of my extended family is in California and New York, so we would take road trips to either coast. We had great times in my uncle's great big Pontiac. He had a Pontiac dealership. We would be in the car for two and a half to three weeks and never once turn on the radio. We just talked all the way through. I love road trips to this day.

All in all, I had a wonderful childhood in Clarkson.

You see, it was a simple life. The Church was dominant. There was a Catholic church and a Presbyterian church. Father Kubesh was the pastor at Saints Cyril and Methodius Catholic Church. When he was not saying Mass, Father Kubesh always had a cigar in his mouth. I served Mass as an altar boy. Little did I imagine that he would counsel me when I embarked on studying for the priesthood.

Maybe the man who had the most influence in my life was Milo Blecha. Because I did not have a dad, he was really a father figure for me.

Milo was hardly more than a farm boy when he trained to be a B-17 pilot in WWII. He flew more than thirty-five missions over Europe. After the war he married and got his teaching certificate. In addition to teaching at Clarkson High School, he coached the basketball and baseball teams. I played for him in both sports. I was too skinny for tackle football.

Athletics were always important in my life, and my coaches were among the best teachers I had. Not long after I graduated, Milo went on to earn an advanced degree and became a college educator and textbook author.

My life was typical for a teenager then. I dated the same girl all four years in high school. A sweet, sweet girl. She and I were very much in love. We were talking about getting married. We frequented the movies and dances at the Clarkson Opera House, which was opened in 1915. It was the site of many receptions and socials and gatherings of all kinds. It had long ago been converted into a movie house, and that is where my friends and I would see movies when we were not driving to Schuyler to catch a show at the Sky Theater drive-in.

My mother and her teaching colleagues staged elementary school operettas at the opera house. It holds fond memories for folks. Big band or swing music was still in vogue then. It was a few years yet before rock and roll became popular.

My life had a familiar routine, and I thought I knew exactly what I was going to do with it after high school. I was certain I was going to go to Creighton University in Omaha to study law. I was sure that I would get married and raise a family. But as I soon discovered, God had other plans for me.

Here's how it happened. I had graduated from high school on schedule and was going about that familiar routine when one day my uncle Joe, whom I still worked for, asked me to go to the nearby town of Dodge to retrieve an automotive part. I was driving a pickup truck on a Saturday morning, about four miles east of Clarkson, when something happened that is still crystal clear to me all this time later.

I distinctly heard a voice say, "Why don't you go to the seminary?" Just like that, out of the blue. I thought, *This is crazy.*

I really did not know what to make of it because the seminary had been the furthest thing from my mind. I mean, it most definitely did not jive with any of my plans. But suddenly, inexplicably, it seemed like a valid option even though it went against all that I envisioned for myself. *Was it God's voice?*

Being a priest is a calling, and I guess maybe it was the call that I felt then and there. If you want to give it a name or try to explain it, then God called me to serve at that moment. He planted the seed of that idea in my head, and He placed the spark of that desire in my heart.

I immediately felt conflicted though because this was during Lent, when there were no dances scheduled, and here I was looking forward to the end of Lent so that my girl and I could go dancing again. I mentioned to her what happened, and she did not say anything about it. So I did not say anything more to anybody else either. I was trying to push it away.

When Lent was over that spring, my girl and I went to a lot of dances just as if nothing had changed. But it had.

Try as I might, the call would not go away. I just could not get rid of it. I could not shake it. I was not much of a prayer then, and so I didn't try to use prayer as an answer. The thing about a calling is that God puts it in you, but then it is up to you to decide if you are willing to accept it or not.

To my surprise, I was willing to consider it even though it conflicted with my best-laid plans. Despite the incongruence of it all, I felt strangely at peace about the whole matter. But I was still betwixt and between about what to do. Then it occurred to me that I should talk to my pastor, Father Kubesh.

When I went to the parish rectory to see him, I announced, "Father, I'm thinking about going to the seminary." He almost fell over.

That was the last thing he would have thought, and he practically said so in his response: "The seminary, huh?"

Father Kubesh and I talked it over a number of times before I formulated in my head the idea that we would never know if being a priest is right for me or not unless I give it a try. So I decided to go to the seminary for one year. It meant I was saying yes to God and obediently trusting in His plan for me.

Father Kubesh and I kept the decision to ourselves at first. Finally, I decided I had to tell my girl and my mom because this was getting serious—I was no longer just thinking about going away to study for the priesthood, I really was going. Nobody tried talking me out of it even though the people in town were shocked when the word got out. They had the same reaction Father Kubesh had—*huh?* It went against expectations. I had a straight shot going into the family business, which is what everyone expected I was going to do. That or go on to school to study law. I really wanted to go to college.

My high school girlfriend went on to marry and raise five children. We are still friends all these years later.

Even though I was raised Catholic, I did not know much about the Church. My uncle and aunt were not Catholics, or at least they did not make a practice of attending church. Joe would take my mom to Mass and pick her up afterward, but he never went inside. But a wonderful man he was—as honest as the day is long. My grandparents never went to church either. My mother was a convert, and, like many converts, she was quite devout by comparison.

All apostolates from Nebraska back then went to study for the priesthood at Conception Seminary College, which is part of Conception Abbey, a Benedictine monastery in northwest Missouri. So that was a slam dunk. Uncle Joe drove me to Conception in the late summer of 1953, and we were no sooner there, then I saw these guys walking around in cassocks. I could not believe my eyes. *Am I going to have to go around in that getup? Am I really ready to do this?* It was my what-have-I-gotten-myself-into moment.

I had tears in my eyes and Joe had tears in his eyes too. My parting words to him were, "Well, I'll give it a shot." And so I did.

SEMINARY:

———————◆———————

I Gave It a Shot

Seminary was difficult from the beginning. I missed all my friends. The studies were hard, although I enjoyed them. I learned to enjoy school very much. I finished my first year and said, "Well, that wasn't bad, I think I'll go back." I ended up going back for nine years before I was ordained.

My first four years were at Conception, and the rest of my training was in St. Paul, Minnesota, at St. Paul Seminary at the University of St. Thomas. The longer I was in the seminary, the more it felt like the right choice, the right place to be.

Father Kubesh and I became close during my years in seminary. Back home each summer, I went to the daily Mass that he celebrated. Afterward we would have breakfast together. We remained good friends up until the time he passed.

In 1958 I came back for the twenty-fifth anniversary of his ordination held at the Clarkson Opera House. Father Kubesh was a role model for me. He was really the only parish priest I knew well at that time. He was great with the people. He was wonderful with kids. He had a delightful sense of humor. He showed me what being a pastor is all about.

Even though I entered the seminary with doubts, and even though my views as a priest have sometimes been at odds with the Church's, never once in my priestly life did I ever doubt the validity or quality of my vocation. A lot of seminarians struggle with this, asking themselves, "Should I go on, should I not go on?" Never once did that kind of questioning ever cross my mind. In my fifty-three years as a priest, I have never thought about walking away from my calling.

Even at the height of the movement when priests were abandoning their vocation en masse to get married—including several of my friends and colleagues—I never contemplated joining their ranks and giving up the collar. I cannot tell you why. I do not know the answer to that other than to say that being a priest has never felt like a burden or a trap to me. On the contrary, it has always felt like a gift.

Of course, things might have been different if I had fallen in love with a woman during my active service, whereupon I would have had to choose between them. This happened to several friends. But the fact is I did not, and therefore that dilemma never arose.

Just as I might have been a flunky working for my uncle Joe, I kept right on being a "flunky" as a priest. I never had any interest in being a monsignor or anything so elevated as that. I am a diocesan priest. The archbishop is my boss.

You automatically become a diocesan priest unless you elect to join the Jesuits or the Benedictines or the Franciscans or one of those orders. I never had an interest in any of those orders. I wanted to work with people in a parish as a pastor. Plain and simple. It is the most direct way a priest can work with people. Parish life is rewarding. It is a family. I am sure my own positive family experience played a part in how I saw my calling being expressed.

My ordination was Saturday, May 19, 1962, at St. Cecilia's Cathedral in Omaha. That was a big moment in my life. Three of us were ordained that day—all classmates at seminary. It was something I had been preparing for during those nine years. I had to take an extra year because, in those days, priests had to know Latin. Some of our subjects were in that beautiful, ancient language, and the Mass then was said in Latin. But having only attended public school in Clarkson, there had been no Latin offered.

I first realized I was a priest when, after the ordination, I blessed my mom and my family. It brought home for me that I was not the same person who walked in. After the ordination, we went to a restaurant to have lunch. I hardly knew Omaha at that time, and in this particular restaurant, female models posed on a catwalk in the dining room. It was awkward to say the least, but we got through it exchanging smiles at the absurdity and incongruity of the situation.

The next day I had my first Mass back in Clarkson. It was a big deal. It was wonderful. As soon as I arrived home on Saturday, I went to the Schuyler hospital and brought communion to a good friend, Anna Husak, a former teacher of mine who was a colleague and close friend of my mother. Anna had been too ill to attend my ordination.

I had made it known to the archdiocese that I wanted to work with the poor. And so for my first assignment as a priest, Archbishop Gerald Thomas Bergan sent me to Winnebago-Macy, an Native American reservation, in far northeastern Nebraska.

WINNEBAGO-MACY:

On the Reservation

Prior to being sent to the reservation, I did not have any kind of orientation to immerse myself in Native American culture. That is the way it is in the priesthood. You get your marching orders and you go. Despite not knowing what I was walking into, the adjustment was easy for me.

Adjusting to any assignment has been easy wherever I have gone. The reason I can fit so quickly into any situation is that I do not have high expectations, and I lead a simple life. I do not judge and I do not demand. My ego is well in check. I know that it is about the people and their needs and not about me and my needs. That trait served me well throughout my service.

I enjoyed working with the Native American people. They are wonderful. I know a lot of them yet today in Omaha. They are simple, they are sincere, they are pure of heart. Unfortunately, they have a weakness for alcohol and drugs that is disproportionate to their numbers in the overall population. That affliction, sadly, leads to addiction and to a multitude of associated problems.

But those problems only apply to some Native Americans. The majority are productive citizens. What struck me about that population and still does today was their gentleness, their kindness, their open hearts, and their deep spirituality.

In Winnebago and Macy (two adjacent towns on the larger reservation), I worked under the aging pastor, Monsignor Frank Hulsman. He had been there for decades. He was a builder. He built the school, he built the parish. He was not so much involved with the people, but he was a productive fundraiser.

Given our age difference, it was hard for us to connect. To indoctrinate myself as quickly as possible, I made a census and went to every home on the reservations. That really helped me to know what was going on. It gave me the opportunity to make a lot of relationships and to reach out to people and let them know I cared for them and loved them.

I was involved with the people in a personal way. For example, Susie White was a parishioner at Winnebago. I was in her home the day John F. Kennedy was assassinated. She was a poor, elderly widow, and I brought her communion that day. She was a devout Catholic, and as we watched television coverage of the tragedy, we both cried at this senseless loss for our nation. Among the Omaha Tribe, I got close to Mary Mitchell. She was the matriarch of a highly intelligent family. She has a son who has taught at the university level.

I never felt as if there was a cultural divide that had to be bridged, though I surely had crossed into a different lifestyle.

Wherever I am, the people are just my brothers and sisters. Of course, every day I was with them, I learned a lot about Native Americans. I am an apt student of human nature. They are a lovely people and they took to me right away.

During my four years tending to the reservations, I lived in Winnebago where we operated the St. Augustine Indian Mission School. It goes back to the turn of the previous century (1909). The mission and school are emblematic of Catholic missionary history. The story goes that elders of the Winnebago and Omaha nations contacted a local attorney to write a letter to the bishop of Omaha, requesting a school be built for their children.

Bishop James O'Connor had been a priest in Philadelphia, where he became the spiritual leader of Katharine Drexel, an American heiress and philanthropist who transformed her life to serve the poor as a nun and later founded the Sisters of the Blessed Sacrament. Her order built and staffed schools for Native American children.

Drexel, who many years after her death was declared a saint, went to Winnebago to personally oversee construction of a church, rectory, and dormitory-school. St. Augustine's was important to the life of the reservation when I arrived there. Kids were coming to the school. The church there had a good reputation. I was part of that whole dynamic, so it was an easy transition for me.

On the other hand, the Catholic Church then was bringing kids into the school and sending them out to white foster parents. Children were discouraged from becoming Native American, from learning their own language, traditions, and history. This was terribly wrong, of course. I encouraged my superiors to allow the children to retain their cultural traditions and practices, which created a stir because it ran up against the thinking of the time.

The idea of Monsignor Hulsman and a lot of priests then was that we had to get Native Americans away from their culture and their language if they were going to be successful, contributing members of mainstream society. In the summertime the kids would be placed with white families in the attempt to break them of the enculturation of their Native ways. That particularly misguided practice caused disruption within Native American families and trauma for Native American children.

Hulsman was really sincere in wanting the Native Americans to become white. He was convinced this was the best way he could help these kids to have a good life. His sincerity and naïveté is no excuse, though, for the damage it did.

Now of course this has really flipped around. Instead of trying to get the Native Americans to move away from their culture, they are encouraged to be more involved in it. Instead of separating Native American children from their families, the families are kept intact. Learning their Native language and ways is supported. Students today are taught to appreciate and adopt these different aspects and traditions of their heritage and identity, which is the right way to do it.

The reservation school now incorporates the eagle feather and incense in the prayers. They combine the Native American culture with the Catholic culture. It is a beautiful thing to behold. The Catholic Church was forced to change its antiquated, arrogant approach because Native American leaders resented the stripping away of their heritage. As the decade of the 1960s unfolded, Native American militancy increased to reflect the protest tenor of the times.

My experience with Native Americans no doubt prepared me for working with poor people of other races and ethnicities and cultures. Virtually all the populations I ministered to lived in poverty, yes, but they also exhibited great love, generosity, and compassion.

I still make it up to Winnebago at least once or twice a year. Kids who were in the Native American mission school when I was there are now providing adult leadership for the tribes. There was a brazen, smart-as-a-whip little girl at the time by the name of Lorelei DeCora. We used to shoot marbles together. She would soon become a full-fledged activist. Even as a child she was brimming with questions and resisting attempts to stereotype her and her people.

She and her mother successfully fought the use of a textbook in the South Sioux City, Iowa, public schools whose depiction of Native Americans they felt was insulting and denigrating. These were among the early rumblings of Native Americans standing on their own two feet to demand respect and to have their voices heard.

A decade later, she called me with an urgent plea, "Father, we need medicine," and pulled me into a mercy mission that landed me in the middle of a fight the whole world was watching at Wounded Knee, which I describe later.

Omaha:

———————◆———————

Racial Tension, Civil Rights

My first assignment after the reservation was Sacred Heart parish in predominantly African-American northeast Omaha, or what was then called the Near North Side. It was 1966 and racial tensions were high. The parish dates back all the way to the 1890s. Then, as now, whites mostly made up the congregation. Some blacks were members as well. The elementary school was just beginning to show the effects of white flight, and within a couple decades, it was virtually an all-black student enrollment.

The new archbishop, Daniel Sheehan, sent me to Sacred Heart to be part of an inner-city ministerial team of priests he put together. There was myself; Jack MacNally, who in a sign of the times later left the priesthood to marry; Jack McCaslin; Jack Killoran; and Terry Finney. Monsignor Peter Dunn of Boys Town headed up our group.

We met once or twice a week, and our job was to report to the archbishop what was going on at a time when so much was happening in the civil rights struggle. We were a group of priests working in North Omaha observing and listening to the heart of the community and then reporting to Sheehan what we thought the Church needed to do to help address this burgeoning social justice crisis.

A grassroots view like that was needed because the Church had really not been there when the cause began, and it was very much trying to play catch up with all that had transpired in the interim, such as the emerging Black Power movement.

The Catholic Church in the United States, as an institution, had a marginal effect on the civil rights movement.

The Church and clergy have always been conservative. Even when civil rights was clearly the right cause, the Church was slow in acknowledging, much less accepting and supporting, minorities. Still, I was surprised by how little the local chancery knew what was going on in North Omaha and by how it did not seem to care until the civil rights movement really began to take hold in the mid-1960s.

I thought the Church would have been involved right from the start, but instead it was detached from these currents until events and laws made it impossible for these social justice issues to be denied or ignored any longer.

Notable exceptions to the Church's indifference were the individual actions of three Omaha priests who followed the conviction of their own personal conscience to get involved rather than follow the hands-off decrees of the hierarchy.

Father John Markoe founded the St. Martin De Porres Club in 1947 as a vehicle for confronting and protesting discrimination. The Omaha group of young people, many Creighton University students, organized some of the first civil rights marches and sit-ins in the nation—centered on 24th and Lake Streets.

Father Jack Killoren pastored St. Benedict the Moor for more than twenty years. In 1969 he built the Bryant Center there, a combined indoor-outdoor facility for recreation and cultural events. When I was given charge of St. Ben's in 2008, the center had fallen into disuse and disrepair, so it was my great privilege to restore and reopen it.

Father Jack McCaslin walked the walk of a civil rights activist by marching in Selma, Alabama, with Dr. Martin Luther King Jr. and by leading a demonstration during a 1968 talk that segregationist and independent presidential candidate George Wallace gave in Omaha. During the 1960s he headed the archdiocesan-run Catholic Social Action Office and used his Sunday Mass homilies at Holy Family Church to decry racism, poverty, and other social ills. He went on to protest the US military war machine at countless nonviolent vigils and rallies. He repeatedly entered military bases and found himself arrested. He is a true model of civil disobedience and a holy man.

Given my own social justice bent, it is little wonder I became friends with the two Jacks. But Jack McCaslin and I became particularly close. I served as his associate pastor at Holy Family for much of the 1970s. We have been neighbors the last few years; we live just a few doors down from each other at a Catholic retirement center.

He is four years older than I, and when I was still a green priest, I looked up to him for his willingness to put himself on the line for his values and to do the right thing even when it meant arrest and getting in hot water with the archbishop. I have tried to follow his example by speaking my mind on controversial issues, regardless of the repercussions.

I am not always in good stead with the archbishop. I got in trouble for this letter published in the *Omaha World-Herald's* Public Pulse the year before Francis became the pope and later offered these same issues for consideration:

It is fifty years since Pope John XXIII opened the windows of the Catholic Church to as he said then "let in an infusion of fresh air—ideas." And as such Vatican Council II ushered the church into the 20th century. The world has changed dramatically over the past fifty years, necessitating Vatican Council III. I recommend that the following topics among others be placed on the table for careful deliberation by the Pope and the world body of bishops. The catechism of the Catholic Church states, each and every marriage act must remain ordered to the procreation of human life. This means that it is always sinful for a couple to use the contraceptive birth control pill, which suppresses ovulation but does not induce an abortion to prevent conception.

Should the Church permit the contraceptive birth control pill to be used under certain conditions?

The defense of religious liberty at home and abroad.

The ordination of women that will provide a new dimension of ministry. Optional celibacy for the priesthood.

Gay and lesbian rights and the pursuit of justice.

How to renew the Church that is in decline in the USA and Europe.

Vatican Councils have resolved contentious issues in the past and made needed changes. Vatican Council III is needed to usher the Church into the 21st century.

The Rev. Ken Vavrina, Omaha

Father Jack McCaslin showed me the way. We were kindred spirits. He has been my hero ever since. He had a huge influence on my life. Other priests became friends along the way but none like Jack. I suppose I might have become friends with Father Markoe as well, but he was much older, and I never really got to know him. But the three of us—myself, McCaslin, and Killoran—were troublemakers in the best sense of the word. We stirred the pot and challenged the status quo.

The Church needed to learn a number of lessons at that time, and some lessons it never learned. There were things I needed to learn, too, such as the white power structure turning a blind eye to North Omaha. Racism was rampant among the power-brokers, and while the Catholic Church sounded sympathetic, I did not think its leaders were sincere.

I am sorry to say the Church was very racist at that time. The Church is often many years behind the times. Omaha's Catholic schools were basically white. Our congregations were white. Blacks were made to feel unwelcome and uncomfortable in our churches. The Catholic Church reflected discrimination in the larger society.

Discriminatory redlining real estate practices and restricted housing covenants effectively prevented blacks from living and moving outside narrowly drawn boundaries. Preferential hiring practices denied blacks many jobs. Exclusionary policies kept blacks out of some establishments or relegated them to the rear. In white churches it was customary for the back few rows to be relegated to blacks. It was indeed a sad situation.

Father Joe Micek, then pastor of St. Richard's, a parish I would eventually pastor in the wake of a scandal, was happy with the way things were. He supported segregation. He got into an argument with my friend, Father Terry Finney, the associate pastor there, over blacks being excluded from the church and from the mainstream.

The only Catholic house of worship in Omaha where blacks felt at home was St. Benedict the Moor. It had been formed to be the city's designated black Catholic church, and it remains that to this day, though things have changed enough that blacks are no longer openly discouraged from attending predominantly white churches.

Thank God that St. Ben's was around when things were less enlightened because it really was a safe haven for blacks. I later served at St. Ben's. It proved to be my favorite and last assignment. Though retired, I am still involved with its Bryant Center Association.

I give Archbishop Sheehan credit for forming the North Omaha Ministerial Team, but it moved too slowly for me. Change was in the air, and the Church had trouble changing to fit the times. It still does. That is just how the Church has moved. I think it is now at an apex where the conservatism is becoming ridiculous. I think there is going to be a trend toward more liberalism in the Church as more people move away from the rigidity of the traditional Catholic hierarchy. The majority of people under sixty years of age no longer attend Mass. Why? There is a confluence of reasons for that. One of them is the Church's intractability. Change is again in the air though. Pope Francis continues to make progressive statements that clearly signal his intent to lead a more welcoming Church that embraces everyone.

Despite my frustrations, working in the black community during the civil rights era was a wonderful period in my life. But I was already beginning to acquire a reputation as a fly in the ointment. I always said what I thought.

By the late 1960s there was much for me to say that upset the apple cart. The African-American community in Omaha's inner city, just like the black communities in inner cities across America, was increasingly angry and impatient for long overdue change. There was widespread poverty and discrimination. Many Omaha blacks had been employed in the packing plants as meat cutters and the like or by the railroads as porters and baggage handlers, but with the closure of the Big Four packing plants and the end of passenger rail service, all those good-paying jobs disappeared.

The schools in North Omaha did not stack up with those in the more affluent parts of town. There was substandard housing, and the public housing projects were becoming high crime areas. Police-community relations were bad. Some cops had a reputation for using excessive force, and the police department and mayor's office did not take the community's complaints about police abuse seriously. Similar complaints about the police have continued through the decades right up to today.

Militant voices for change were being raised, and I got to know some of these activists. Charlie Washington was a journalist who told it like it was in the *Omaha Star*. I was at plenty of community meetings with Charlie. He was a tough guy, very single-minded. He just plowed through it all. But he was political enough not to burn bridges.

The younger, brasher Ernie Chambers, on the other hand, did not care whose feelings he hurt or who he alienated in getting the message out that change was needed by any means necessary. Ernie used Dan Goodwin's Spencer Street Barber Shop, where he worked as a barber, as his bully pulpit. He was featured there at his eloquent, needling best in the superb TV documentary *A Time for Burning*. He went on to serve multiple terms in the Nebraska Legislature representing the majority African-American District 11.

He was my barber when I was at Sacred Heart. He cut my hair and bent my ear many times. I have always liked Ernie. I thought he was right about most things. He really reaches out to the disadvantaged. If I ever got into a jam, he was the first person I would ask for assistance because he is sincere. Smart as hell too. But he is his own worst enemy because sometimes he says things that make it difficult for him to get things done. But he is always forthright and says exactly what he thinks. I am one of the few clergy Ernie hit it off with, maybe because I was not afraid to speak my mind either.

I also got to know *Omaha Star* newspaper publisher Mildred Brown, activists Dorothy Eure and Buddy Hogan, and many others on the front lines of change. They all helped me to better understand what was going on in North Omaha. That is how you learn—by listening to the people.

Then there were the Black Panthers. Two Black Panther Party members, David Rice and Edward Poindexter, were well-known figures in the community. Rice, now known as Mondo we Langa, was a Creighton University student and the director of music at Holy Family. He also wrote for two underground newspapers. Ed was a Vietnam War veteran.

They formed something called the National Committee to Combat Fascism that was essentially the local Black Panther Party chapter. They advocated the creation of fair housing and ending racism in the Omaha Public Schools. They promoted political education and worked to end the Vietnam War. As a show of support, I became a member of the organization. They referred to me as "the blackest cat in the alley." I was always on the street. They knew whose side I was on. My support of the Black Power movement just came automatically, it was just natural.

There had already been civil disturbances on the north side. At the end of a hot day in the summer of 1966, a crowd gathered in the evening at 24th and Lake, the hub of the black business district then. When police ordered the crowd to disperse, some folks grew angry and things escalated to the point where cars and storefronts were damaged over the next few days.

That same summer, riots erupted after a nineteen-year-old black man was shot by a white, off-duty policeman during an alleged burglary attempt. In March 1968 a crowd of high school and university students, some organized by my friend Jack McCaslin, went to the Civic Auditorium to protest George Wallace's segregationist stump speech. Counter-protesters got into it with them.

By the time the police waded in, dozens of people were injured. The melee spilled outside and ignited a larger disturbance that caused much property damage. An African-American youth who just happened to stumble into the situation was shot and killed by an off-duty police officer.

So you see, things were already at a boiling point. Some businesses suffered such losses that they closed and never reopened. Other shopkeepers abandoned North 24th Street out of fear of future trouble. Anything viewed as unjust was likely to set off segments of the community again. And then it happened.

In June 1969, police officer James Loder went to the Logan Fontenelle projects in response to a call about a disturbance. It turned out to be just a bunch of kids playing loud music in a vacant apartment. As soon as Loder pulled up in his cruiser, the kids ran away. But for some reason he aimed his revolver and shot fourteen-year-old Vivian Strong at the base of her skull and killed her. She was unarmed and posed no reasonable threat. Rioting broke out that night.

Per police protocol in an officer-involved fatal shooting, Loder was suspended. He also faced possible manslaughter charges. For his preliminary hearing I was at the courthouse with many others from the community. The judge did nothing to him. He was free to go. Those of us there to see some sort of justice served were angered.

On my way back to the rectory, guys were handing out leaflets on how to make Molotov cocktails. That night, North 24th Street burned. It burned from Hamilton to a little ways north of Binney Street, a swath of some fourteen blocks or so, north to the south. And I mean it burned.

Businesses were torched. Only charred shells were left. Total losses. Windows were broken. There was looting. The street was packed with so many people that fire trucks and ambulances could hardly get through. I was on the street helping to clear the way for the first responders. Sacred Heart parishioners hosed down the roofs of the rectory and the school to protect them from the blowing embers. The rioting took place for three nights. All of it precipitated by the judge being so ignorantly lenient with the police officer, who was never convicted of anything.

Those were tough years. It is not as volatile now, but North 24th Street has never come back. Some fire-ravaged buildings and others untouched by the fires were abandoned. Some were razed, and others just sat there before being torn down. On many tracts, nothing went up in their place, thus leaving a scarred landscape of vacant lots.

There has been some new in-fill. You can see some progress at 24th and Lake and 24th and Grant and even as far south as Patrick and Hamilton Streets. But north of 24th and Lake remains quite untouched. There are many good people working to revive the area and just as many plans for redevelopment. But it is taking decades and generations to accomplish, which is far too long for me and many others to accept.

What saddens me is that I left for overseas in 1977, and when I got back nineteen years later, Omaha's inner city showed little improvement and in some ways had taken steps backward. The great new scourge was illegal drugs and gangs. Sections of northeast Omaha became controlled by gangs. That new reality has hurt the community.

There is an epidemic of black kids getting shot and killed by other black kids, usually over money or turf or revenge. The drive-by shootings often result in innocent parties being shot. How sad. These kids have no idea what they have been given by those ahead of them who suffered and even died in the struggle for equality. All they are thinking about is their money in their pockets and their false sense of pride and their short-term gratification.

The poverty is as bad or worse than before. Unemployment and underemployment among blacks is far too high. Too many young people are dropping out of school. The sexually transmitted disease rates are off the charts. Too many children are having children. Thousands of single mothers are struggling to get by. The number of black men arrested and incarcerated is overwhelmingly disproportionate to their percentage of the general population, which speaks to a law enforcement and criminal justice system that unfairly profiles or targets African-American males.

We must encourage young people to stay in school. It is a challenge though because so many come from broken families, and there is not the steady, positive, reinforcing adult in their life to steer them the right way. Then there is the hopelessness many people feel. They do not see how an education is going to help them. They cannot see themselves in a job and earning a living wage. They cannot visualize a way out or up out of this mess, which is why some turn to drug dealing, stealing, or prostitution.

Fortunately, organizations like the Empowerment Network, the Urban League, and Girls Inc. as well as churches, foundations, and other nonprofits are working to address disparities and to place people on pathways for success in education and employment. I serve on the board of an organization, the Bryant Center Association, which is one of many in the black community working to give youth positive alternatives to the street.

What today's organizations and initiatives are doing is not so different from what yesterday's were attempting. But because of the tense tenor of those earlier times, all sorts of well-intentioned folks fell under suspicion. Law enforcement kept a close eye on anyone who was even remotely considered a threat to the state.

Operation COINTELPRO or Counter Intelligence Program encompassed covert projects conducted by the Federal Bureau of Investigation. Government agents infiltrated antiwar and civil rights groups. The key word is *covert* or secret, which means at the time we did not know the program existed.

But it turned out Black Panthers Mondo we Langa and Ed Poindexter, myself, and several others here and countless more people around the country were under surveillance, sometimes illegally. An event happened that later brought all this to light.

Omaha police officer Larry Minard was killed and officer John Tess was injured in August 1970 when a suitcase containing dynamite exploded in a North Omaha home they had been called to. It was a trap.

At that time, I was teaching school at Rummel High School (now it's called Roncalli), and about a week after the tragedy, I came home from work to find two FBI agents waiting for me at the

Sacred Heart rectory. They were looking for Mondo and Ed, who were suspects in the bombing. An informant had incriminated them. The authorities were questioning me because they knew I was a friend of these guys. Mondo was a dear, dear friend.

The feds showed me a file an inch thick they had collected on me. They knew all kinds of things about me and my personal affairs. They had apparently bugged my office or wiretapped my phone. They thought I might know where Mondo and Ed were, but I had no idea of their whereabouts.

The two men were eventually found, arrested, and charged with murder.

From the start, they proclaimed their innocence. At trial they were convicted even though the evidence against them appeared weak, and there were allegations of police and prosecutorial misconduct. They have been serving life sentences ever since.

Many observers then and now believe in their innocence. Some assert they were framed by the COINTELPRO operatives. Groups have mounted various efforts to have their case reopened and retried, all to no avail. Their men's many parole appeals have also been denied. By the way, the two of them have been model prisoners all these years. I have always meant to visit them in prison, and I will do that one of these days. I pray they get their day in court again or else a judge commutes their sentences and grants them their freedom.

My first decade or so as a priest saw much fraying of the American fabric. Civil unrest, assassinations, Vietnam, the drug culture, the sexual revolution, women's liberation, gay rights, Vatican II, priests and nuns leaving the Church in droves, the Watergate conspiracy with Nixon eventually leaving office.

I could have despaired, but I never had any doubts about my vocation. I never experienced the dark night of the soul Mother Teresa and other deeply spiritual people have described undergoing. I am not that holy, I am not that spiritual. It helped that I never had great self-expectations. I think I inherited that from my mother. She was that way. It also helps me to have lots of friends. As my favorite saying goes, I never met a stranger.

WOUNDED KNEE:

———◆———

"Father, we need medicine."

My next stop after Sacred Heart was at Holy Family, where my dear friend Jack McCaslin pastored. With our similar progressive views, we were like two peas in a pod.

Located in what is now called North Downtown or NoDo, Holy Family was maybe the first Omaha church to radically incorporate Vatican II liturgy. We had a lively liturgy. The congregation was filled with people who were sort of in the vanguard of what the church should be doing. The Church went through numerous changes moving from the Latin to the vernacular. I loved it. So did Jack. Some priests had a hard time with that changeover.

The first time I was suspended came while I was at Holy Family. A friend of mine was divorced and looking to get remarried, but he was not able to get an annulment, which meant he could not be married in a Catholic church. So he was married in a hotel. I went there and said a prayer for him and his bride, whereupon I was scolded by the chancery office. They took away my faculties to officiate any weddings for six months.

The Church strongly discouraged divorce at that time and could make it difficult to get an annulment. Jack and I were sympathetic to the tough place that put people in. We were also sympathetic to the plight of minorities. We tried to welcome them into the Church they so often felt rejected by. For example, we welcomed African-Americans at Holy Family. We also both had a heart for the gay and lesbian community, and we tried to have a gay and lesbian Mass. It never really materialized.

During his papacy, Pope Francis, who is a humanist like me, has clearly indicated in words and tone his wanting to include divorced Catholics and gays and lesbians, among other marginalized people, into the full embrace of the Church. The more he openly talks about the need for the Church to care for all people, the closer to reality a fully inclusive Catholic Church will be. It is an encouraging development.

In the late 1960s through the late 1970s, many friends of mine left the priesthood to get married. As for myself, I never thought about doing that. I was at Sacred Heart at the time this phenomenon really started to kick in.

Jack McNally, the pastor there at the time, left and got married, as did many other wonderful men. These were great guys I knew well. We are still good friends to this day. I understood why they were doing it. They fell in love and wanted to be married.

Most of them were disenchanted with the priesthood anyway. The priesthood is not an easy life. Some of them were not good at preaching, and they simply did not want to do the job or to follow the call anymore, although they continued doing good works and serving their fellow man, but not as priests. Besides wanting to marry, there were many reasons why these men left the priesthood and, in some cases, left the church as well. There is rarely only one reason why any of us does anything.

After Mass at Holy Family one Sunday in the winter of 1973, a young Native American woman whom I knew when she was a girl on the Winnebago Reservation, Lorelei DeCora, phoned me with an urgent plea. She was calling from Wounded Knee, South Dakota, in the middle of an ongoing siege making national and world headlines.

What became a seventy-one-day uprising began when a group of some two hundred Oglala Lakota and members-followers of the radical American Indian Movement (AIM) occupied the town of Wounded Knee on the Pine Ridge Indian Reservation on February 27. AIM had done this sort of thing before, such as occupying Alcatraz Island, as a platform to air Native American grievances about second-class status. But this protest was more aggressive and the site of it even more symbolic because in 1890 US troops perpetrated the Wounded Knee Massacre there.

The organizers of the occupation were the Oglala Sioux Civil Rights Organization (OSCRO) and AIM. They established the Independent Oglala Nation and demanded the US government's recognition of the 1868 Fort Laramie Treaty with the Sioux Nation, the removal of the Oglala Sioux tribal council, and new elections.

The seizure was the result of long-simmering intertribal tensions between passive, conciliatory leaders and more militant activist camps led by AIM, and clearly the militant faction won out. Some of the Native Americans who controlled the town were armed, although the vast majority were not.

Women, children, and elders were among the occupants, and it remains unclear to this day whether all were there of their own free will or not. The activists made several demands, most having to do with improving poor conditions on reservations and seeking redress for historical wrongs committed against Native American peoples. Virtually every treaty Native Nations entered into with the federal government had been broken by the United States.

After the activists gained control of the Pine Ridge Reservation town of Wounded Knee, South Dakota, federal, state, and local law enforcement officers, led by the US Marshal Service, cordoned off the area. The marshals and other agents occupied the high ground on the surrounding bluffs. They wanted the Native Americans to come out and give up their weapons and provide their names.

The Native Americans insisted they would not leave and flatly refused to give up their guns and names. Tensions ran high. During this intractable confrontation, regrettable, tragic mistakes were made on both sides. Shots were fired, especially at night. Eventually, people were injured and killed.

Lorelei was an enrolled member of the Winnebago tribe, Thunder Bird Clan. Her great grandmother had survived the 1890 massacre at Wounded Knee Creek, where federal troops committed atrocities. Lorelei had attended the St. Augustine Indian Mission School on the Winnebago Reservation when I was there, and that's where her activism first surfaced.

She resisted efforts going on for Native American students to abandon their cultural traditions. She became a youth representative to AIM's national board of directors. Through that organization she became involved in the larger Native American protest movement and took part in the 1972 Trail of Broken Treaties caravan to Washington, DC.

She was nineteen when the siege at Wounded Knee played out. She took on the role of medic, nursing people with wounds incurred in the gunfights that broke out. She went on to become a nurse. Her advocacy for Native American causes has found its full expression as a health care provider. She later founded the Porcupine Clinic at Pine Ridge.

The occupation attracted major media coverage. Many Native American supporters traveled to Wounded Knee to join the protest. It was amid this chaos that Lorelei reached out to me with that frantic phone call to say, "Father, we need medicine."

It was sometime in mid-February, only a couple weeks into the standoff, but the children and older folks were sick and in need of supplies. The Native Americans inside the compound were unwilling or afraid to ask the agents surrounding them for this assistance—angry at them for being under assault and fearing they would be shot if they tried to leave the area they were billeted in.

As soon as I got off the phone with Lorelei, I called a Native friend of mine, Joe Yellow Thunder, an Oglala Sioux. I explained the situation to him and ended with, "Joe, let's go to Wounded Knee."

I arranged with physician friends at old St. Joseph Hospital (now Creighton University Medical Center) to provide me with quantities of medicine. I loaded my car with the supplies, and Joe and I drove off to Wounded Knee the next day.

It all happened so fast that I didn't give a lot of thought as to how we would get the supplies into a raging armed conflict, much less past law enforcement checkpoints. I trusted God would guide us to our intended destination.

Wounded Knee lies in a valley, and once we reached the rim, there was an armored personnel carrier right in the middle of the road facing the vehicles coming in. We stopped as directed, and I said to the guard who approached our vehicle, "I've got medicine for the Native Americans. I need to get down there."

I was told, "No, you can't go down there. You have to go to Whiteclay and get permission to go in there."

So we drove to Whiteclay, a speck of a Nebraska town near the South Dakota border and almost within spitting distance of Pine Ridge. Whiteclay has earned an infamous reputation for selling ungodly amounts of alcohol to the Native American population, thus exploiting and enabling their predisposition to alcohol addiction.

Joe and I found the appropriate authorities encamped there. They were using the town as a base of operations. After much conversation and a thorough inspection of our vehicle and the supplies, to make sure we weren't sneaking in weapons, we were allowed to go into Wounded Knee under cover of a white flag affixed to the car antenna. I was under strict orders to deliver the medicine and get out.

What I came upon in that town under siege was a surreal scene. AIM leader and cofounder Dennis Banks, whom I knew from before, was there, and we greeted one another. Dennis held a walkie-talkie in one hand. He was in charge.

We knew each other because interestingly the American Indian Movement had come to Omaha months before. Dennis

Banks, Carter Camp, Vernon Bellecourt, and Russell Means had all stayed in the basement of Holy Family Church for several days while Means went through court proceedings in Omaha for possessing a gun in a Nebraska jail. So I got to know all these guys at that time.

Upon greeting me at Wounded Knee, Banks said, "Father Ken, I want you to stay here. We need a witness."

Every night the Native Americans were shooting at the marshals, and the marshals were shooting back at the Native Americans. Both sides were blaming the other for starting the shooting. Banks didn't want an atrocity repeated there without someone he trusted to bear witness.

I explained to him, "I don't have permission to stay here." Then I saw Lorelei and I looked her in the eye and asked, "What are you doing here?"

She said with great conviction, "I came to die."

They really thought they would all be killed. They were fully committed. On his walkie-talkie Banks reached the authorities and relayed his desire that I stay there as a credible, neutral observer. He told them, "Let this guy stay here. He's objective. He'll let you know what's going on."

The authorities went along with his request, and that's how I came to spend two nights at the compound. We bivouacked in a ravine where the Native Americans had carved out trenches. We used straw and blankets over our coats, plus body heat, to keep warm at night. It was not much below freezing, and there was little snow on the ground, which made the camp bearable.

At night the shooting would commence. I had never seen a tracer in my life until then. Fortunately, nobody was hit while

I was there. On my last day at Wounded Knee, the marshals gave permission for the Native Americans to come out into the open without giving their names or surrendering their weapons. This was a huge concession by the authorities.

There was a big powwow led by the holy man or spiritual leader, Leonard Crow Dog, who was from the Rosebud Reservation. We went to the top of the hill where the graves are of the people who had died in the 1890 Wounded Knee Massacre. The Native Americans got out the blanket and the peace pipe and prayed. I was the only white person present. They thanked God nobody had been killed in this current conflict.

Before I left, I did communicate with the marshals through Dennis Banks to report what I had witnessed, including the tracers going overhead at night, the Native Americans huddled for cover, and several of the occupiers sick with cold and flu symptoms.

Once back home, Joe and I attempted to make a second medicine supply run up there. We drove all the way to the rim but were turned back by the marshals because the violence had started up again and had actually escalated. When the siege finally ended that spring, there were many arrests and a whole slew of charges filed against the protesters.

About six months after Wounded Knee, Leonard Crow Dog invited me to a sacred sun dance ceremony at Rosebud. The young Native American men who participated had fasted for a few days in a sweat lodge in preparation for the ceremony.

When it was time, a tribal holy man pierced the skin on each man's chest with a piece of bone attached to a long leather strap. The strap was tied to a hoop ring affixed to a tree or pole. The sun dancers invoked the power of the sun as they moved forward until they pulled far and hard enough that the bone popped out of their chest. Most fell to the ground in pain, and the holy man healed the wound with a handful of dirt. It left a nasty scar.

It was a whole day of piercings and pulling skin. This purification rite was a sacrifice for the tribe. It was a solemn, serious ceremony, and I was honored to be there to witness it.

Hundreds of people had been arrested at Wounded Knee. They were variously tried in federal, state, and tribal courts. Lawyers from across the country organized the Wounded Knee Legal Defense/Offense Committee (WKLD/OC) to represent the defendants. Among them was Lorelei DeCora. The AIM leaders, including Dennis Banks, faced the most serious charges. The Committee also handled cases related to protests and resulting arrests at Scottsbluff, Nebraska, and Custer, Rapid City, and Sioux Falls, South Dakota.

The Committee also brought civil suits against several authorities, including the Oglala Sioux tribal council and its president, Dick Wilson, and the FBI.

Because it was determined that it would be impossible for the defendants to obtain a fair trial in South Dakota, the trials were moved to other states, including Nebraska, where federal district Judge Warren Urbom presided over many cases in the capital city of Lincoln. Due to a lack of evidence and prosecutorial misconduct, the vast majority of charges and cases were dismissed.

Lorelei had all her charges dismissed. She moved to Pine Ridge, where she has been a community leader. Dennis Banks, who surely has nine lives, went underground for a time to avoid serving a sentence handed down against him. He was given sanctuary and reinvented himself as an educator, author, and actor. He eventually did serve time.

SOUTH SIOUX CITY:

Longing to Become Unimportant
Doing Christ's Work

After Holy Family, I went to St. Michael's parish in South Sioux City, Nebraska. It was 1976, and this stop turned out to be my final assignment in America before going overseas.

My experience at St. Michael's was completely different than my preceding experiences with African-Americans and Native Americans because I was serving in a white parish in a growing Latino community. People from Mexico and Central America had begun moving there to work in the large meatpacking plants in nearby Dakota City.

This was my first time around Latinos in a sustained way. My only previous exposure to Spanish speakers was on a vacation to Mexico during my Holy Family tenure. I do not speak Spanish, but I speak Latin and I know a little bit of Italian, which, like Spanish, is one of the romance languages, and so it has similar grammatical roots. I led a Spanish Mass at St. Michael's, which was a big change for that old-line Anglo parish. Because the younger Latinos in the parish spoke English, there was no real language barrier in my dealings with those families.

I was one in a long line of non-Latinos to serve the parish. Only recently did South Sioux City get its first Latino pastor, and he was only the second in the entire Catholic Archdiocese of Omaha. There is obviously a need for more Latino priests in the archdiocese, where the number of Spanish-speaking Masses has exploded because of the large influx of Hispanic immigrants. These new arrivals naturally want priests who not only speak the language but also understand their culture.

During my stay in that northeast Nebraska town, I became restless. I felt I was out of the mainstream, away from the action. Plus, I knew the civil rights movement was petering out. I knew it was not going to reach what I thought it could achieve. I was disappointed it would fall short of its potential.

So I decided I was going overseas. I wanted to be where I could do the greatest good. I always felt drawn to the missions. Chalk it up to that sense of wanderlust I first felt as a boy. I just felt a need to experience voluntary poverty and to become nothing in a foreign land.

I initially thought about going to South America, but some travel I did to Hong Kong, Thailand, and Singapore on vacation from my St. Michael's duties—I had found an airline-hotel package deal—got me thinking about another part of the world.

Specifically, an experience in Thailand changed the whole trajectory of my missions plan. I was walking the streets of Bangkok, which is a real tourist town, only I was on the edge of downtown, making my way down a paved road. Then I made a wrong turn and suddenly found myself in the slums of Bangkok.

I had never seen conditions like that in my life. Certainly I witnessed nothing to compare to it in Omaha or in any of the other places I pastored. It was an overwhelming experience to be immersed in those slums because everywhere I looked was human want and suffering at a scale I was unprepared for. I saw absolute, abject poverty. People lived in overcrowded huts that had no electricity or running water. Children ran around dirty and hungry, some of them emaciated and clearly starving. I kept on walking and observing. I must have spent several hours just taking it in.

I was shocked and appalled by the conditions people lived in. I realized there were slums all over the world and these people needed help. What was I doing about it? The experience really hit me in the face and marked an abrupt change in my thinking. I looked at my relative affluence and comfortable existence, and I suddenly saw the hypocrisy in my life. I resolved then and there, I was going to change, and I was going to move away from the privilege I enjoy, and I would work with the poor.

I was bound and determined to do that, and that is exactly what I did. I regard my sudden commitment to follow a radically different path another calling from God.

There is no doubt God led me to the missions, but I was also heavily influenced by the example of two religious figures I greatly admired: Mother Teresa left behind the well-off life she enjoyed as a girl to become a nun who eventually dedicated her life to serving the poorest of the poor. Cardinal Paul-Émile

Léger shed his privileged life as a leader in the Catholic Church in Montreal to work with lepers.

The following words spoken by Mother during her visit at Boys Town in 1976 resonated deeply within me: "The greatest disease is not leprosy, the worst disease is to be unloved, to have no one who cares."

As I came to know, she must have said that same thing a thousand times or more. I also often heard her say, "The greatest poverty is to be lonely and unloved." That is what she would tell people who wanted to come to Calcutta, but she reminded inquirers that there are a lot of people right in their own parishes who need help because they were alone and unloved.

When she made that appearance at Boys Town she was already well known. I had read a biography about her, *Something Beautiful for God* by Malcolm Muggeridge, which became a documentary. Both the book and the documentary made a huge impact on me. I was moved and inspired by her unabashed devotion and commitment to the poor. The die was already cast that my path would cross with hers in service to the poor.

Sometimes when a priest goes off to the missions, people think, "Oh, he's in trouble." But I was not running away from anything. I enjoyed the priesthood, I enjoyed everywhere I worked. No, I was running toward something—in this case, a simpler life that would put me in intimate contact with the most needy human beings on the planet.

At that juncture I had already worked in the archdiocese fifteen years, from 1962 to 1977, and I loved every minute of it. I was finishing up a master's degree in counseling at Creighton

University. Everything was good. No nagging doubts. But I just felt compelled to do more. I thought I could be of some help to the Missionaries of Charity and their founder Mother Teresa, who was a great inspiration to me. I received permission from the diocese to work overseas. I made the announcement of my missionary work at the end of May 1977 and left July 13 that same year.

I remember when I talked to my family about my impending departure, my mom cried. Her first reaction was, "You're going to go hungry." Here is a letter I wrote her about this life-changing decision:

Hi Mom,

I have asked and been given permission by Archbishop Sheehan to work as a foreign missionary. I shall be going to either Africa or India this summer, most probably India. I know this comes as a surprise to you but not to me. I have been thinking about it for years.

One of the reasons for my coming to St. Michael's was that learning Spanish would aid in my work in a Spanish-speaking country. I am leaving it up to the mission office and the chancery to determine where I shall go. Priests are needed most in India, secondly in Africa. I am corresponding with both countries' foreign missions.

I am not anxious to go, as I like it here, and I know it will be hard in a foreign country. But I have been saying no to the Lord for too long a time. I have finally said yes. I know that you and

Ron are not happy with my decision but there is
no doubt that it is God's will, so I will be okay. I
am healthy and still young.

I had no regrets then, and I have no regrets now. I had a longing to become unimportant doing Christ's work. I think subjugating the will and deflating the ego is the source of great happiness. When not encumbered by things is when you are most happy and free. Perhaps that's why that one-year leave of absence the chancery gave me to do foreign mission work turned into nineteen incredible years helping the poorest of the poor.

YEMEN:

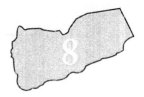

———————— ● ◆ ● ————————

The Leper Village Known
as the City of Light

When Archbishop Sheehan granted my request to serve overseas, I was directed to London, where the Missionaries of Charity had a presence. I arrived there only to find out the order's European center was in Rome. That is where I could find Mother Teresa, I was told, which I was highly motivated to do, and so I went to Italy.

My first meeting with Mother was memorable. She visited me after Mass as I was eating breakfast. Throwing her hands up in the air—she always threw her hands up in the air—she said, "Oh, Father, thank God you're here. We need a priest in Yemen to work with our sisters in the leper village. Would you be willing to go to Yemen to work alongside our sisters with the lepers?"

I simply replied, "Sure."

The reason I jumped at the request without hesitation is that this is precisely what I left the United States to do. I was prepared to accept any opportunity to be of service, even if it meant working with lepers in a country I could not find on the map. She explained that the priest who had been at the leper colony in Yemen had contracted hepatitis and had to be medically evacuated out of the country.

After getting my visa and travel clearance—Mother Teresa even accompanied me to the Yemeni embassy in Rome—by that evening I was aboard a plane on my way to an Arabic land. I indeed traveled back in time, as our pilot sarcastically announced on approach for landing in the Yemeni capital of Sana'a, "Be sure to set your watches back three hundred years."

The full import or truth of that statement did not hit me until I was living there and saw how women were treated.

Catholic Relief Services (CRS) had an office there. Somebody picked me up at the airport and took me to where the Peugeot station wagons were waiting outside. Peugeot wagons are ubiquitous modes of public transportation in many parts of the world, including Yemen.

About ten or twelve of us shared the cab ride to the highlands city of Taiz, near where the leper village is located. It is about a five-hour drive from Sana'a to Taiz. In Taiz I was met by two of the sisters from the leper village who took me to the hut with a dirt floor that became my home.

When I sent a letter to my mother telling her that I was to be working with lepers, she was, of course, alarmed. It was probably the last thing she expected her youngest son to do. But in time she accepted it as something I had to do.

Because things did move so fast, there was no time to be briefed in any detail about Yemen or lepers before leaving, except Mother Teresa did impress upon me that Yemeni and Muslim law forbid me or the sisters or anyone else to proselytize for Christianity under penalty of expulsion or worse. And as soon as I arrived, the sisters filled me in on all the dos and don'ts and most definitely reinforced what Mother had said. In order for us to remain in that country to do our work, we absolutely had to abide by these restrictions.

Mother Teresa visited Yemen shortly after I arrived there. Like wherever she went, her visit caused quite a stir because everyone wanted to see her and touch her. People came out of the woodwork and practically knelt at her feet.

Father Ken, about age forty, an eager young priest,
arrived to serve the leper colony in Taiz, Yemen.

Mother Teresa got involved as a result of Catholic Relief Services' intervention there to provide food for starving refugees from Ethiopia. The Ethiopians were, like the lepers, a minority group being discriminated against. CRS got the word out about this humanitarian crisis, and Mother heard about it in Rome. She went to Yemen to visit the leper village. After seeing the sad state of things, she agreed to send her sisters to work there. Mother had a real affinity for Yemen.

Mother told me that before she arrived in Yemen, the Yemenis tried burning down the leper village in an effort to get rid of what they regarded as an unwanted and expendable population. They would not have anything to do with the lepers or so much as touch them. They would not even get close to them. So it was either have the Missionaries of Charity come in to care for the lepers or leave the lepers' fate in the hands of a hostile government and general populace.

What people fear and do not understand is what they turn against. The lepers desperately needed an advocate who could be a buffer between them and the public and authorities. By giving Mother and her sisters permission to go in there, Yemeni officials did not have to bother again with the lepers. It was, as the saying goes, "Somebody else's problem." Plus, the lepers could rest more easily when not harassed, expelled, or harmed.

In 1963 a building to shelter people with leprosy, those who had been rejected by their families and friends, was constructed in a village about two miles outside of Taiz. Physicians visited regularly to diagnose cases of leprosy and to recommend the treatments in use at that time. What was originally called the leprosy center or leper village was given the name City of Light by Mother.

During my time there it was officially just outside Taiz's city limits, but it has since been incorporated into the city. It was not far enough away for the comfort of the Yemenis. They wanted the leper village farther away or gone altogether.

The fact that Mother got the Yemenis to agree to let her sisters in was a real coup because Yemen had for a long time been a closed society that did not welcome foreigners. By the time she made the deal, Yemen was still somewhat suspicious of outsiders. The country did not readily welcome foreigners because Yemenis wanted to retain their Muslim traditions. They did not want foreigners to interfere with what they thought was a great life.

Tradition there elevates men far above women, who inhabit a subservient position. The men have the world by the tail. All a Yemeni man needs to do to leave his wife is say to her, "I divorce you, I divorce you, I divorce you," and, just like that, he and his wife are divorced. He gets to keep the boys, she gets the girls, and he can get another young wife. The fundamentalists do not want their patriarchal, male-dominated lifestyle to change, so their attitude was, "Stay out of here, mind your own business, leave us alone, we're having a great time doing things our own way."

When Mother Teresa and I had a moment or two to ourselves, she explained that the leper village had been in such dire conditions before her sisters took charge that the lepers were actually matted to their blankets due to the drainage from their sores. The sores were not being treated properly, nor was the bedding being changed regularly. The patients were not being taken care of at all satisfactorily. Mother said she had never seen a situation like that in her life where the people were so ill-kept. It was a crying shame and a terrible disservice to these poor people left to suffer.

I did not know much about leprosy other than what I had read years earlier about Father Damien, "the leper priest" whose work with those afflicted in Molokai, Hawaii, eventually earned him sainthood.

I knew it was a contagious disease, called Hansen's disease, that it was not present in the United States, and that for a time there was no cure. The disease exacts a horrific toll on the human body by causing disfiguration, open sores, nerve damage, and death.

I also knew there was a good deal of misinformation and many myths about it that made people afraid at even its mention. That fear led to much of the discrimination (and worse) against lepers. I myself was not immune from believing some of these stereotypes at the start.

The resident population was highly superstitious. They felt if somebody became a leper, it was because their father had committed a sin. In other words, as a son you were being punished for the sin of your father. It is only with knowledge and experience, faith and understanding that we overcome our fears.

In those years there were conflicting North and South Yemen states. South Yemen was a communist country. Cuban troops were in South Yemen fighting the north. There was always a war going on between the north and the south. Instability came with the territory. Their unification into the Republic of Yemen that exists today did not happen until after I left. As with so many nations in that region, unrest remains an ongoing issue, and the rise of terrorists and extremists has only contributed to more instability.

Ultimately, I can only describe my introduction to the City of Light as a shock.

YEMEN:

———— ◆ ————

Learning the Joy of Service to Society's Outcasts

You cannot imagine what it is like going to a leper village for the first time. The fear is palpable and darn near paralyzing. I did not take my hands out of my pockets the first day. I was scared to death of contracting the disease. I literally walked around all day with my hands buried inside my trousers.

I observed things and got a feel for the place and for the routine there. I must admit though that I kept a distance from everybody. The second day, the third day, the fourth day, the same thing, only I was becoming a little braver, a little less paranoid with each exposure, and slowly but surely letting my guard down. By the fifth day I was acclimated. I was no longer afraid. I do acclimate quickly no matter what the situation. The people there helped me to adjust to life in a leper village. After about a week, I felt at home.

A leper village is an environment all its own. It is truly another world. Because I did not speak Arabic, their preferred language, I learned to communicate nonverbally, with a smile, with my eyes, with hand gestures. My communication with the patients went haltingly at the beginning. The sisters had to help me. None of the Yemenis spoke English at all. They were from the bush area, from little remote villages, and so they spoke their local dialects.

Thank God the sisters spoke English fluently. Often a sister would help me to know what to do. Eventually I picked up enough Arabic to get by on my own. Relatively quickly I acclimated to that completely different way of life.

Even apart from the way lepers were forsaken by their families and communities, there were other harsh realities I had to come to terms with in that desert land. For example, public executions are still in use there, and I did witness an execution by stoning. A young man accused of raping a boy was buried in sand except for his head. A notice had been put out announcing his public execution, and a crowd gathered in the open market for what transpired.

Soldiers threw stones at the man's head until they thought he was either unconscious or dead. Then one soldier took a sword and cut off the man's head and hung it from the main gate to the open market where everyone could see it. The head hung there by the hair for maybe five months. It was intended, of course, as a deterrent.

Making peace with such brutality was part of acclimating myself to the culture I was in. Like it or not, resigned to or abhorred by what I saw, there was no thought of intervening in a situation like that. Any attempt by me to do so would have resulted in my arrest and expulsion. I did not want to give them an excuse to kick me out of the country.

As the stoning and beheading played out, I reminded myself, this is what they do here, this is the way it is, this is how they have done things for millennia. It is none of my business. I also reminded myself that we still have capital punishment in America. Depending on the state, America executes its condemned by electric chair or lethal injection. Yemen has stoning and beheading. Not that big a difference. Killing is killing.

There were four Missionaries of Charity sisters running the leper village. They were trained as nurses, and specifically they were trained to work with lepers. They filled me in on everything. We were careful to wear rubber gloves when we were in contact with blood. I learned that you can get leprosy

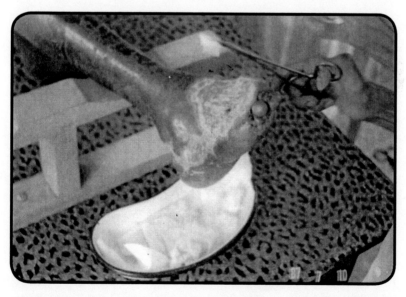

This is the type of work I did with lepers, carefully scraping the dead skin. These are probably Gemila's hands. She is not wearing gloves. We wore gloves to do this work.

the same way you get a cold, through exposure to coughs or sneezes, but the most likely way of getting it is if you have a cut or an open wound and you touch an active leper. That is why we wore rubber gloves. As a precaution, I wore the gloves all day every day when I was working with lepers.

There was a woman I worked with there by the name of Gemila. She was a leper herself. She was testing negative by then, which meant the medicines she was taking were working and she was no longer an active leper. Therefore, she was able to work with lepers and nonlepers alike. She was a single mother whose child lived with her in the City of Light, where she had resided for several years. She was smart and sweet as sugar.

As time went by, I established deep bonds with the lepers. They became my family. I loved them. Gemila and I worked as a team with lepers. I loved her as a friend.

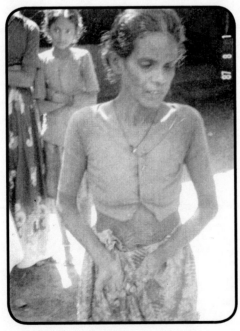

My sweet Gemila, a leper who tested negative, she assisted us in Taiz at the leper colony with the care for other lepers. Her hands were horribly crippled. She sadly died after I left Yemen.

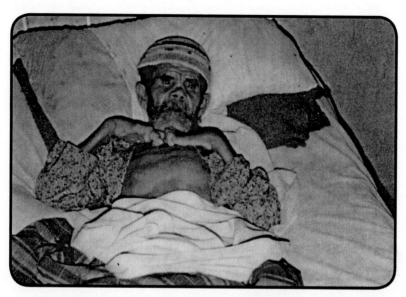

A man in Yemen who had leprosy. He would beg at the side of the road.

Active lepers were not permitted to beg or to leave the compound. One man always ran to the road. He had girlfriends he would go off to see. He would beg at the side of the road. We did not permit people to beg. If they were negative, like Gemila, we let them out, but he was active; he was testing positive for leprosy. He died during my time there.

In the City of Light alone, we had more than three hundred lepers, including two hundred fifty active cases. Many were coming and going, though, and so it was hard to be precise with numbers. We did not have facilities for more than three hundred people in the City of Light. Because we had more people than beds, the excess would sleep in the open.

I myself slept in the open all summer—on the roof or on the ground because it was so blazing hot, even at night. When you are living in the desert, the temperature in the summer gets to one hundred and ten degrees or more. The heat rises

Poverty and leprosy were causes for the poor and downtrodden in Yemen to sleep on the streets and beg for food.

quickly from the sand. It picks up small particles of dust, and then, when it cools down at nighttime, the dust comes down. When you wake up in the morning after having spent the night outdoors, as I did, you find yourself covered in this fine dust.

In addition to the City of Light, we operated a mobile leprosy clinic where we would go into villages in a jeep and treat lepers on site where they lived. Frankly, we went to them so they would not come to our village. Here's the problem: once they came to our village, we could not get them out; they just would not leave.

Why should they have left? For perhaps the first time in their lives, they were comfortable and accepted, they formed friendships, and they had girlfriends and boyfriends. But that did not change the fact we had limited accommodations, and overcrowding posed more dangers to everyone's health. So we would treat lepers as best we could in their own villages.

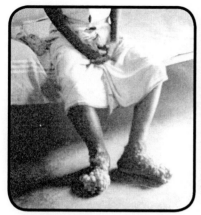

In the villages we also saw Yemenis with elephantiasis, an incurable disease caused by parasitic worms that afflicted one in eight people.

I do not know what Gemila's relationship was with her family, but if it was anything like that of most lepers, then it was estranged. Typically, the family would separate themselves from a leper. Harsh as it sounds, they did not want to associate with the afflicted, loved one or not. Lepers were absolutely ostracized from family and society. Having a leper in the family was a stigma. It would reflect badly on the entire family. Siblings, even though disease-free themselves, might have trouble finding suitors or spouses because they were related to a leper.

There is no sound basis for any of this misconception because most people have a natural immunity to the disease, and lepers treated with today's medications do not need to be isolated from society.

Lepers have always been outcasts. Generations ago, people with leprosy in Yemen, as elsewhere, would often be separated, willingly or not, from the rest of their family and community because of the fear of contracting it. In fact, leprosy is not that contagious as long as you take proper precautions. In Yemen,

A young man with leprosy. Men were more likely to get leprosy. Women were usually covered and protected.

lepers retreated into caves near the villages where they were born and raised. Historically, people with leprosy were sent to leper colonies on remote islands or put in special hospitals. Things only began improving for lepers in the second half of the twentieth century.

Mother Teresa formally handed over another leprosy center in Taiz to the Yemeni Ministry of Health. In 1998 three Missionaries of Charity were killed by a mentally ill person in Hodeidah, but the order continued its mission in Yemen. Today, the City of Light houses the National Hospital for Dermatology and Venereology and Leprosy. The work of the sisters and others expanded leprosy care and research throughout the republic. Many leprosy clinics were opened and new multidrug therapies greatly reduced the number of cases.

While the number of facilities and the drugs to treat leprosy improved, attitudes proved harder to change. In my time there, efforts to educate the populace about the disease proved daunting. We were battling a lot of negative traditions and perceptions. We tried to help people be reasonable in their decisions and to accept the lepers when they tested negative. We encouraged families to welcome loved ones back into their homes and villages. But there was much resistance. Old habits and ways of thinking die hard.

More men than women lived in the leper village. Women are generally at less risk of exposure than men because women are covered all the time and stay in the house much of the day, and so they are not as susceptible to direct contact with lepers. Also, the hygiene of a man is not as good as the hygiene of a woman.

Females from the underclasses did not have much formal education. A peasant father would never send a girl to school because it was viewed as being an economic loss to the family. They use a dowry system. You lose your daughter to the family of the man she marries, and the father of the bride pays a dowry to the father of the groom. It is a disincentive for a father to ever invest even a penny in a daughter. So women really have a hard life there.

The lepers did most of the work in the City of Light. They were the best at doing this work because they had gone through all this themselves. They understood, they empathized, they were fearless. They were the ones who really guided me as to what needed to be done at the clinic. My primary job was to scrape dead skin off patients using a knife or blade. It was done very crudely. Lepers, whether they are active or negative cases, have a problem of rotting skin. That putrid skin has to be removed for the affected area to heal and to prevent infection. After performing a scraping, I would then clean the skin.

I would also keep track of the lepers and where they were with their treatment and the medicines they needed. When we were running low on meds, I would make sure to get our order in to Germany, where the Catholic Church distributed free leprosy drugs around the world. I would go to the American Embassy in Taiz to use the telex machine to send our orders for a new supply. The order would come to Djibouti, Africa, and then on to Taiz.

The red tape in Yemen was endless. You needed what seemed like a thousand signatures. It was necessary to grease the wheel with customs agents to get our order released and prevent it from being delayed or diverted or held back or somehow misplaced. In other words, I needed something to bribe the agents, all of whom were men.

A friend of mine named Ted Moore, who was from England, worked for an international engineering company in Taiz. He sympathized with my plight; therefore, whenever I was going to Taiz to retrieve the next shipment of meds, he provided me a *Playboy* magazine as enticement for officials to cut that red tape. All I had to do was open my briefcase and give an agent a flash of that *Playboy* cover, and, whoosh, the meds were whisked through and into my possession.

Men are so predictable that way. If Mother Teresa only knew what it took to get those meds through, she would have fainted. On second thought, I suspect she would have laughed and accepted that corruption is just the way things are done in developing nations.

I am sure more than once she or someone in her circle violated rules, if not laws, to get what she wanted. I am sure she struck under-the-table deals and dealt with less-than-sterling characters. Indeed, later I saw her at her manipulative, expedient best in India when she needed a CEO's assistance to get supplies airfreighted somewhere. It was just one of many examples I saw of her practicality and tough-mindedness.

Meds were not the only supplies we received from outside the immediate area. The Catholic Relief Services office in Sana'a was a major source of food to feed the poor, the lepers, and the African refugees fleeing civil war.

Advanced leprosy cases sometimes required amputation. This is particularly indicated when plantar ulcers or severe bone/joint disintegration occurs. You have to extract fingers and hands and feet and often noses because, otherwise, gangrene sets in. You have to get rid of these infected appendages. The operations were often performed without anesthesia because

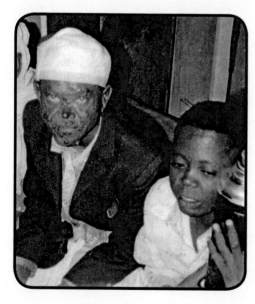

This man lost his nose to leprosy at our leper colony in Yemen.

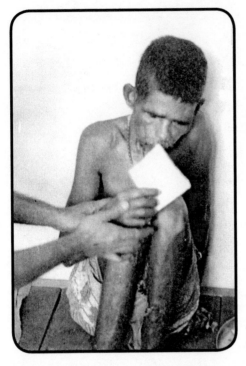

The ravages of leprosy, Yemen.

leprosy attacks the tissues and the nerves, thus leaving patients with no physical sensation of pain.

We would bring in doctors to do examinations and to perform amputations. My duties required me to be present during these procedures, which I observed. As hard as it may be to believe, I got used to seeing fingers and noses removed. Once, a doctor removed a man's foot just above the ankle. As difficult as that was to watch, it made it easier when I realized this was good for the man because, by having that appendage removed, he would no longer be an active carrier of leprosy. He was going to probably become a negative leper and therefore be able to go outside of the leper village and mingle with the regular population again. That, after all, was our objective.

The leprosy drugs of that era were not nearly as effective as the ones that later came into use. Thanks to better drugs, leprosy is much reduced in the thirty years since my experience in Yemen. Sadly, a lot of the lepers we worked with died. Another factor in improving outcomes is that health workers have been able to get villagers to practice better hygiene and to let go of their superstitions. As a result, there are fewer new leprosy cases today.

One of the sisters I worked with contracted leprosy. She took the prescribed medication, and thank God she was able to get rid of the disease. At that time if you could catch leprosy at its earliest stage, it could be cured; otherwise, no cure was possible. Once you got it, you had to live with it, and the best that you could do was to become negative. A blood test could easily determine if you were negative or not. Blessedly, I never came down with leprosy. I checked myself a lot and the symptoms never appeared.

However, I didn't escape medical issues entirely. I contracted malaria in Yemen. I got it within a week of my arrival. A mosquito bite was the culprit. Americans as a rule do not have any resistance to malaria because we have not lived in these climates. The Yemenis and the Africans, for example, are able to resist malaria because they inherit a tolerance to it. By contrast we have nothing in the way of resistance when we go to these countries. We are vulnerable. The same with diarrhea, as I discovered to my distress.

There are inoculations to prevent malaria, but I did not take them on the good advice of others. It was explained to me that if you regularly take malarial prophylactics and you live in a disease prone area, as I did then, the drugs can damage your hearing and vision and can make you immune to the meds, thus rendering them ineffective. Instead, my colleagues and

I waited until we had a malaria attack, and then we took the medicine, thereby making it more potent.

Early in my stay in Yemen, I toured various villages one day and found myself feeling poorly. I did not know it at the time, but I was feeling the telltale first symptom of malaria—a headache in the back of the neck. The nerves bunch up there and it hurts. That is how a malaria attack starts. Later symptoms include fever, diarrhea, and vomiting, if it gets that far. Many times it has gotten that far with me.

Like many undeveloped countries, Yemen is a place of contradictions. The people of Yemen are fiercely capitalistic, shrewd businessmen, and entrepreneurial. Yet cultural customs hold the country back from realizing its full potential because the education of girls and women is discouraged. That bias against women denies Yemen and countries like it a whole segment of intellectual and entrepreneurial capital.

One of the biggest lessons I later learned in India is that when you have a chance to educate a girl, you educate an entire village. As I witnessed for myself, that dynamic is possible in India, where it is more of a matriarchal society, but not so much in Yemen, where men rule absolutely and women are mere chattel.

There is also a gaping disparity between the rich and poor in Yemen, as there is in India and Liberia. That kind of vast socioeconomic gap only used to exist in Third World nations, where I saw it firsthand. As an aside, it now alarms me that the gulf between rich and poor in America is so enormous these days and ever widening. A class war is brewing that threatens our democracy.

A precious resource equally scarce in Yemen, regardless of class, is water. Water shortages are felt by rich and poor alike, though if you are rich, you can at least import more water than the natural environment provides. When I was there, though, there just was not enough clean water to go around. After the rainy season in July and August, a donkey cart brought water to the houses every three days. This was at best good for one shower. With water at such a premium, I learned to take sponge baths.

In order to carry out my duties at the leper village, I was required to have a work permit, which meant I had to get a real job. So I managed to get two jobs while I was there, The first was teaching English and math in an English-speaking elementary school in Taiz, where I worked mornings. The school had boys and girls. The Yemeni women teachers on staff were the exception to the rule by virtue of their considerable education and their Western attitudes. They confided to me their displeasure with the severe constraints women lived under there. They really let me know what they thought.

By Yemeni standards, these were avant garde, outspoken women. They had higher education, which meant they had progressive fathers who permitted them to go to school out of the country. So these were unique women from elite families, and the kids who went to our private school were from privileged families as well.

My first two years in Yemen, I taught at the school but that ended when the Yemeni authorities decided having a non-Muslim teach the children went against the Koran. The headmaster wanted me to stay, but he was getting pressured to let me go. Fortunately I was able to get a new job with the local purchasing office of Hanab-Stefen, a Dutch-British engineering firm in Taiz that was putting in some roads and a sewer system. They employed a number of Dutch and British workers, one of whom would play a critical role in the final days of my Yemeni experience. I did purchasing for the company over telex lines.

My daily routine became rather fixed. I got up at five o'clock every morning. I still do. You had to get water from the well about a block away because there was no running water. It was a communal well free for all to use. In a bucket I would retrieve the water I needed in order to wash or to boil for drinking and cooking. I had to boil and filter the water to make it safe to drink. When it is really hot, the water settles and worms appear on top. I would scrape the worms off. Despite boiling the water before using it to drink or cook with, I still got dysentery from those worms. I could write a book on diarrhea.

My hut was outfitted with a gas canister. I attached a hose from it to my hot plate to fuel it. That is how I boiled the water, and it is what I cooked and warmed food in.

I would have Mass in the Mother House at 7:30. The sisters would prepare breakfast for me afterward. A typical morning meal would consist of eggs, some sorghum, and some bread. The sorghum was cooked in a liquid and served like rice. Other dishes contained lentils and rice and often featured a hot-as-hell little bean that gives a pungent taste. For many of the dishes we used bread instead of a spoon or fork to scoop up the food.

The sisters would take me to the school in their jeep, and I would teach there until 11:30. Then a kid on a motorcycle would take me to the leper village. I would ride on the back of the bike, holding onto him for dear life. I got burns on my legs from the exhaust.

Traditional stone homes in Yemen. Mine, nearby,
was made of dirt with a floor of dung.

At the City of Light, I worked with lepers until about
6:00 or 6:30 p.m. Then the sisters would take me to the souq,
the big open market. We had to buy our food every day
because there is no electricity for refrigeration. I would buy
only what I was going to eat that evening. I would generally
get vegetables, sorghum, beans, sometimes fish because we
were not too far from the sea. As soon as I got back to my
hut, I cooked what I brought home from the souq. That was
a daily ritual.

I remember one time I was cooking something in a pot,
and I was sure there was a cockroach in it, and I went ahead
and ate it anyway. I was that hungry. Besides, insects contain
good nutrition. Lots of protein.

The open-air market or souq where I purchased my evening meal daily because we had no way to keep fresh food refrigerated.

The souq is a lively place, with merchants manning their stalls hollering and vying to get your attention. It is the social place or center of the city. That is where people go to sell things and buy things. Free enterprise. Haggling is part of the deal. Shoppers have to haggle everything to get a halfway decent price. You never buy at the first price they tell you. Because I was an American, they jacked up the price they quoted me tenfold. Yeah, they took advantage of me, that was understood, but I think I fared all right.

To get anywhere, I either fetched a ride or I walked. I wore out several pairs of sandals tramping around Yemen. Whenever I would go from Taiz to Sana'a, I would go via a Peugeot station wagon for a white-knuckle ride in the mountains.

These drivers were crazy as hell, and to make matters worse they chewed khat, a flowering plant that when ingested puts you in an altered state. It is a mild hallucinogen and narcotic. Khat seemingly grows everywhere in Yemen and seemingly everyone there uses it—men, women, youth. It exudes a green juice.

Once, on a flight from Taiz to Sana'a, the pilot exited the cockpit, and judging from his blurry eyes and the green streaming down his mouth, it was immediately obvious that he had been chewing khat while he flew the plane.

The one and only time I tried khat, it gave me constipation. That was enough of a deterrent for me to lay off the stuff.

The simple life there agreed with me. Women sold cow dung for the Yemenis to layer on their huts' dirt floors. It hardens like cement and emits an odor that keeps the bugs out. The Missionaries of Charity did not pamper anyone and they certainly did not pamper me. I had nothing but the contents of two suitcases in my possession. I slept on the floor. No electricity, no running water. When the heat or the wind or the rain became too much, I rolled down bamboo curtains.

Mother Teresa did not cater or kowtow to any of her volunteers. You were given nothing, you were on your own. You lived in poverty the same way she did.

On the rare occasion when she visited Yemen, all the routines went out the window. As I later witnessed, it was the same when Mother went out into the streets of India or really anywhere she appeared. Her mere presence set off a buzz that caused people to stop what they were doing just so that they could come get a glimpse of her or perhaps touch her. She was that admired and revered.

We needed to expand our humble hospital facility in the leper village where surgeries and amputations were done. We needed a better facility, but Mother came and said, "No the first thing we're going to build is a mosque. We have to build a mosque so people can pray to God."

Her decision and conviction to do that was characteristic of her independent, unconventional thinking. But as I also witnessed, she could be quite stubborn and a real autocrat. Sometimes her single-mindedness was to a fault.

All the time I was in Yemen, I was the lone Catholic priest in and around Taiz. The only other priests I saw during my years there were in Sana'a and in the port city of Aden, and they were White Fathers, a missionary group from Ireland. The Irish make great missionaries. They can go to these horrible situations and retain a great sense of humor. Because they have the temperament for it, they survive wonderfully.

If any of the White Fathers favored a spot of whiskey or a bottle of beer, they were bound to be frustrated because Yemen is a dry country—meaning the sale and consumption of drinking alcohol is illegal there. But, as I found out, if you really wanted something, you could find a way to smuggle it in or get it on the black market.

Now, I do not drink myself, but I fell in with some fellows who arranged a system for bringing alcohol in from Djibouti, Africa. I let them persuade me one time to go to the Yemeni port city of Mocha to fetch their illicit shipment of booze. The way they worked it out was they paid somebody to stow away a quantity of whiskey and other spirits aboard a regularly scheduled supply ship from Djibouti. Then someone else was paid to remove the crate from the hold and take it to a designated spot in the desert, where they hid it behind a sand dune. I was given directions where to go.

I drove out there and, of course, one sand dune looks like the next, but as I went around this dune and that dune, I finally spotted the crate filled with several bottles of Johnny Walker whiskey. That bit of intrigue in the desert was my chance to play Lawrence of Arabia.

Mocha, boy, that is the armpit of the world. During the summer, every afternoon, like clockwork, there is a sandstorm, and the sand is just an all-enveloping, driving mass that penetrates and irritates everything in its path. You cannot escape it. Unless you are in it, you cannot imagine the discomfort. For starters, it is hot as hell, and then this strong wind off the sea picks up the sand on land and blows it with such force that you have to cover your nose and your eyes. It is blinding and smothering. You feel you are going to suffocate. There can be so much sand that sometimes the drifts are deep enough that cars get stuck in them.

Which is what happened when a leper landowner asked me to drive him into an outlying city so he could buy a pickup truck and drive it back. We rented a Peugeot station wagon to go to Hudaydah, where we picked up his vehicle. We started driving back to Taiz in a two-car caravan when this sandstorm suddenly came up and enveloped us in a storm of earth that blotted out the sky. We promptly got stuck in a drift.

Not wanting to be buried alive in that hot sand, we got out of our vehicles and thankfully nearby found a house that we walked up to and asked for shelter. The family was kind enough to let us spend the night there. The next morning, we had to dig our cars out of the sand with shovels so that we could complete the trip back home. It took a good while to free them. Mind you, this was that landowner's first driving experience, so I have to think it was a memorable one for him as well.

My stay in Yemen was not all work. My greatest adventure there had to be the time I hiked up the fabled Mount Kilimanjaro, a volcanic mountain that sits on the Tanzania-Kenya border. I just decided I wanted to go to the top of this highest mountain in Africa (its peak measures out at 19,341 feet above sea level) made famous in books and movies. It represented another bridge to cross.

I flew to Ethiopia and then into Tanzania. It was August 1980. I have always kept fit, and I was jogging a good bit in Yemen, therefore I felt confident I was in good enough shape to make the hike. Once in Tanzania, I secured the services of a guide. For this hike there was me, the guide, and a rock climber from Switzerland. I had to rent all my gear.

We started out at 5,000 feet. That first day we went to 7,000 feet, which is where the ascent really got started. From there we came upon a beautiful rain forest teeming with life. I could just feel a million eyes of animals and insects peering at me, the most obvious of which belonged to these big black monkeys. The next day we climbed above the frost line. From 7,000 feet to 12,000 feet, we slept in tents at night.

On the third day we trekked up from 12,000 feet to about 15,000 feet. By then we were above the tree line. We went to bed and got up about midnight and the guide said, "Okay, let's go," and the three of us hiked all night in the pitch dark, the guide ahead of us, the guy from Switzerland and myself trailing him, climbing a mountain by flashlight. It was probably just as well that I could not precisely see our narrow trail or the precipitous drop-offs around me.

Going up, we met people coming down who were saying, "Boy, it's cold up there." We had to really be careful because at the first signs of hypothermia, you start shaking and it saps all your energy. I said to the guide and to the other climber, "Let's walk all night and just stop once because we don't want to start shivering." So we stopped one time to rest and to eat some cold biscuits and to drink hot tea.

Then we walked again until we reached Uhuru Peak (the highest summit on Kibo's crater rim), which is the rim of Kilimanjaro. We got to just below the top of Uhuru before the sun came up. When I saw the peak ahead of me, I almost ran up there. Then, still not atop the summit, I made the mistake of sitting down, whereupon I started to vomit and get dizzy. I managed to take some pictures of the sun coming up. I wish I had those pictures but I cannot find them.

I still had about 350 meters to get to the summit. My head was spinning and I was not well. The path led straight up a glacier and then straight down on the other side. Somehow, I made it to the top. I had a picture of myself and the guide at the top, but it has been misplaced. There is a book at the summit in which you sign your name along with any inscription. I wrote my name and "Deo gratis" or thanks be to God.

I was proud of myself because I went right up that mountain like a goat. My mission complete of having "conquered" Kilimanjaro, I began the long trek down. It should have been easier going back down only it turned out my shoes were too tight, and I had developed blisters on the way up. Walking down the mountain with blisters proved very painful. But all in all it was a wonderful experience.

As an aside to that trip, on the flight back, the plane was not able to go to Sana'a as scheduled. Instead, it was diverted to Aden, the capital of South Yemen. I spent a fitful night in a hotel there because on a regular basis there were military planes flying overhead and bombing on the border as part of the ongoing North-South Yemen conflict. I could hear the thud of explosions.

I joined some men at the hotel for dinner and discovered I was breaking bread with military personnel who piloted those planes on those bombing sorties. I said, "Please don't drop those bombs on me in Taiz." They laughed. It turns out they were Soviet pilots working for the South Yemen government. That was the one and only time I made it to Aden, and I was glad to get out of there.

Five years into my Yemen sojourn, I was quite content with my life and work. The lepers taught me so much about faith, love, humility, and gratitude. Shunned and rejected by so many, they found among each other a community of kind and compassionate hearts and kindred spirits. The sisters and others who worked at the City of Light taught me the joy of service, of giving, of doing unto others what you would have them do for you. I learned the lesson of simplicity, of how removing all extraneous things can bring one closer to God and to your own true self.

It is why I shave my head the first of July and the first of January. I have for decades. It is emblematic of my unconcern for my appearance. In a place like Yemen or India or Liberia, it is easier to ignore the external trappings of vanity that come with hair and clothes but I have maintained that discipline all through my travels, onto my return to America seventeen years later and right on through to today.

Being so far away from home and separated from familiar rituals and traditions, I was susceptible to the tug of nostalgia and emotion. On one of the Christmas Eves I spent in Yemen, I had been working all day with lepers in that harsh, taxing environment. Then I had gone to the souq to purchase my food for the night.

When I got to my hut, I lit a candle and I turned on my transistor radio to the BBC (British Broadcasting Corporation). The BBC was my eyes and ears to the world. Fortunately they were broadcasting King's College Choir from Cambridge, England, with scriptural readings and with beautiful music. As I was listening on that Christmas Eve night, I wept. I will never forget that. I still break up just thinking about it.

In many ways Yemen was the place I found the most contentment. Then, late in 1981, without warning, everything in my peaceful, well-ordered world changed when I suddenly found myself an enemy of the state. Nothing could have prepared me for what happened next.

YEMEN:

———◆———

I Just Got Out of Jail

For my nearly five years in Yemen, I was anything but the Ugly American you sometimes hear references about when US citizens go to a foreign land and disrespect or disregard another country's customs and laws.

In my work with lepers, I was cognizant the whole time of the strict rules that foreigners like myself must follow in heavily Muslim Yemen. I faithfully abided by the restrictions laid down for us, and I never once violated those boundaries. As a standing policy, we could not permit any Yemeni national to attend any of our Catholic religious services for the sisters. Even if a Yemeni wanted to go to Mass just out of curiosity, we had to turn them away.

We were also expressly forbidden from doing evangelization work. Therefore, I never spoke about Christianity to the people there. In fact, I never spoke about religion at all to any Yemeni, not even to the Christian Yemeni.

That is why what happened came as such a shock. I was in the leper village one late afternoon, and somebody from the state security force arrived unannounced wanting to see me. I was in the building where I did a lot of my work when this agent presented himself and told me in abrupt, no uncertain terms that I had to submit my documents immediately. This occurred with no warning whatsoever. I knew all my documents—my visa, my passport, my work permit—were in order, so I had no idea what this could be about. It was just so out of the blue.

I was ordered to go to the local security office that night in downtown Taiz on the pretext that my documents needed to be examined. I got to this small office around 6:30, and then all hell broke loose. As I sat in a chair, I was surrounded by stacks of files in boxes. A security officer sat in a chair on the other side of a desk.

On the surface it seemed to be some record mix-up, and I was there to help clear up the problem. But it soon proved to be an interrogation. I ended up being questioned—grilled, really—for four hours. This was some intense business. It became evident the government officials were curious about me.

As the evening droned on, they wanted to know what I "really" was doing in Yemen, apparently convinced my work with lepers was some kind of cover for espionage. Indeed, they implied or insinuated I was working for the CIA, which could not have been further from the truth. My only controls were God and Mother Teresa, in that order.

None of that seemed to impress or deter or placate my interrogator. He was a young Yemeni man who informed me in English he had just returned from London where he said he studied security methods. He probably wanted to show his stuff in this investigation. Oh, boy, did he ever ask me a lot of questions.

My mind raced with possible reasons for why I was in that hot seat, being treated as a suspect. Exactly what I was suspected of doing, I could not fathom and they did not say. Then my interrogator described something that apparently triggered my being targeted.

There were maybe a dozen Peace Corps volunteers working in Yemen then. Among them was a young woman, a recent graduate of Rutgers University, assisting us with the lepers. She attracted attention because, by Yemeni standards, she dressed provocatively—favoring tight Western-style clothes, which was a breach of local tradition. It was an insult or sin as far as the Yemenis were concerned.

A male Peace Corps volunteer drove a motorcycle, and "that woman" often rode on the back of his bike with a black veil trailing her. It was not only a spectacle but a spoof of Yemeni customs, which was a terrible thing to do. These same volunteers would go all over the place snapping photos in areas near where there were active skirmishes between the North and South. When the couple got too close to the border, they were arrested and accused by the North of taking surveillance images of sensitive military installations.

My interrogator pressed me about this woman and my relationship with her and her colleagues. He asked, "Why is this woman taking photographs when we understood she is here to work with lepers?"

He kept asking, "Why are you here? Why is an American working with lepers?"

It evidently mystified them that an American would willingly choose to work with lepers for as long as I had. This suspicion was no doubt fueled by their own prejudice and fear when it came to lepers. My interrogator also repeatedly asked if I knew this person or that person, such as the headmaster at the school I taught in. Well, the headmaster was a good friend of mine, so of course I knew him. Every person he named, I knew.

I knew a lot of people in Taiz. After all, it had been my home and workplace for five years. I believe he was trying to discover that I had been proselytizing to these people. If there was one thing they would have liked to have pinned on me, it was that. They were always alert to that and to any attempt by Christians to make converts. In Islamic law there is almost no greater sin than for a Muslim to become a Christian. We never did that, period. I was careful not to go into homes where it might appear to outsiders I was cultivating converts. I followed every propriety and edict.

He kept hammering away with the same questions. I did the best I could answering them and keeping my cool in that hostile and nerve-wracking situation. I recall that a couple other men came into the office at a certain point, and they were jotting everything down I was saying.

It proved to be the first of four consecutive nights of interrogation.

I was released to go back to the City of Light after that first session, but they brought me back the next night to answer more questions for a second session, and they repeated this process. The interrogation was complete after the fourth session, but this ordeal was far from over, as I was placed on house arrest. It meant I was able to live in the leper village and have Mass with the sisters as before, but then security would escort me to the office where I did purchasing work part-time. Then I would be brought back to the City of Light to work there, and at the end of the day, the sisters would drop me off at the souq. So my routine really did not change all that much.

My house arrest lasted three months. I just could not understand this treatment. Even with all of the restrictions and questions, I did not think I was in any real danger or trouble. I felt they were just going through these security protocols as a precaution. I sincerely thought this mix-up or misunderstanding would all be cleared up soon enough. I figured it was just a matter of time before they dropped the investigation and lifted these restrictions and I could go back to living and working in freedom.

But my naïveté was shattered when one day an investigator came to the leper village to tell me I was being summoned to the capital city of Sana'a to defend myself against charges that I was distributing Catholic materials.

The American Embassy knew about my having been interrogated and put under house arrest. Their staff told me right off that Yemeni security was going to put me in jail. The authorities never said that, but at least I had a heads-up as to what I could expect. The security people told me they were going to have a detail meet me at a jitney stand where all the taxis lined up to take me into Sana'a.

The American Embassy urged me to have someone I trusted accompany me to the rendezvous point to act as a witness in case I went missing. I asked Mick McCartin, who worked for Hanab-Stefen, to come with me. Mick was from Ireland. He had a family back there. He and I became good friends. He used to serve Mass for me when we had Mass for the expatriate community. I got to know the expats quite well.

Mick loved soccer. He loved to drink. The embassy insisted all precautions be taken to let them know where I was being taken. I explained it all to Mick, how I was in this predicament or pickle and that I needed him to note the make and license number of the vehicle I was put in. As soon as I was taken into custody, his job was to go back to Haban-Stefen—this is before cell phones—to fax the ambassador the particulars.

The security team met us as planned, and I was promptly escorted from Mick's vehicle into an unmarked van. Mick and I exchanged glances as he drove off. The agents secured chains around my wrists and put me in the back with another man in custody. I learned he was from Turkey but I do not know what he was accused of. At least one of the security officers brandished a gun. It was some sort of automatic weapon. The journey into Sana'a was a rough four-and-a-half-hour ride. None of us spoke much. What could we really say?

I distinctly remember that, as we approached the outskirts of Sana'a, a Land Rover, with whom I presumed to be a big Yank behind the wheel, started following us, which told me Mick succeeded in informing the embassy. As usual the streets of Sana'a teemed with camels and goats and people. In all that jam-packed crush of activity, the American tailing us was not able to keep up or else lost sight of us.

In any event, I was alone again with my captors. We went around a corner, then inside a gate, and the gate closed behind us. Every home or business compound was gated in Yemen at that time because there were no property rights in effect, so a gate was the only thing protecting you from someone seizing and claiming your place as their own.

There was no such thing as a formal jail. There were just secure buildings where people were housed under guard.

We entered a three-story building. The Turk and I were led to an area on the ground level with a dirt floor. They put us in a locked, windowless room maybe the size of a small classroom filled with other prisoners. There might have been as many as fifty of us in that room. There were so many detainees that not everyone could lie down at the same time. We had to alternate standing and lying down. At least there was some basic ventilation to move some of that stale, fetid air in and out.

The Turk and I were the only expatriates. Everybody else was a native Yemeni. Some were political prisoners from the South. Some were rebels accused of trying to overthrow or undermine the North's regime.

I remember talking to the guards and asking them, "Why am I here? Tell me—why am I in jail?"

None of them said anything. They probably did not know themselves. The most I could glean during the whole experience was that I was suspected or accused of distributing Christian materials, though they never presented any evidence of this activity. I was never actually officially charged with a crime. In their minds, suspicion was enough to hold me and badger me.

Even though I personally felt relatively safe as an American citizen, in the background we could hear occasional screaming and gunshots. Men were being tortured and executed. None of us knew with any certainty our own fate, but I never allowed myself to think the worst.

Now that I was incarcerated, I figured I was going to be there six months. I prepared myself mentally and emotionally for that likelihood. I calculated that after that point everything would be okay, and I would be released. But in the eventuality that things did not go according to plan, I conditioned myself to expect that I might even be there for some time beyond that.

You may find it hard to believe, but I never worried. I just knew that everything was going to be all right. I knew that being an American often carried weight in such matters involving foreign governments. I thought that was a plus for me. I trusted the American ambassador and his people would eventually locate me and either get me out or intervene to move things along. I also had confidence in knowing I had done nothing wrong, I had not violated any law. My faith in God is what ultimately made me feel so serene in such a hard, unsettling circumstance.

It did not take long to get used to the routine in jail. We were all given a thin mat just to keep us off the dirt. It was winter time, and even with the mat, it was hard and raw and cold on the floor. I already had a little bit of arthritis in my back, and by the time I finally regained my freedom, I was stooped over.

They fed us once a day, usually in the evening. The guards put a big dish of vasulia on the floor. It is made from sorghum, the main crop they raise in Yemen, and eggs beaten all together to make a mush. It is flavored or spiced with a very hot pepper. Flatbread was also provided. You would tear off a piece of bread and use it to scoop up the vasulia.

In the morning our jailers would let us out of the room we were all cooped up in overnight to go outside in the courtyard, where we could stretch out and walk. It also gave us a chance to squat and go to the open-air "toilet." Back inside the close quarters of that small room, we peed in bottles the rest of the time. Besides the foul smells that could be nauseating, the drinking water was polluted. I got very bad diarrhea. There was no place to go, and I really stunk up the whole jail. That was the situation day after day after day for ten straight days.

Guards periodically came in to check things over. One of them was sadistic. He liked to hit people for his own perverted sense of sport or pleasure. An incident involving that guard and me took place a few days into my confinement.

A wealthy, well-dressed, immaculately groomed man from South Yemen named Abdullah was brought into the jail. Some of my fellow prisoners had heard of him. He was a Sheck (landowner) whose holdings made him an important person. He immediately attracted a lot of attention because he was like a star in our wretched midst. His influence bought him three or four mats to sleep on.

Shortly after that, another Yemeni prisoner was brought in. Unlike the privileged gentleman, the new arrival was a man of humble caste and means like the others. Seeing he had no mat to sleep on because the rich man had more than his share, I said, "Abdullah, why don't you share one of your mats with this gentleman. He has no place to lie down."

Abdullah became very angry with me. He let everybody know he did not like me. He even let this be known to the police-security duty. The sadistic guard came in the next morning carrying a rifle, and Abdullah told him I should be punished because I "worshiped the devil." Those were the exact words he used in Arabic.

I was lying down when this guard came up to me in a way meant to intimidate me. He was incensed. I thought he was going to hit me with the butt of the rifle. I stood up and we both noticed that he was a full head shorter than I. I stood just as tall as I could get, towering over him, and I looked down and stared at him, and he looked up and stared at me. I do not know if he felt intimidated, but at least he did not hit me or harass me. He gave me one more look, then turned and left without saying a word.

That was the only time I felt any real danger or sensed that I could be injured. I do not scare easily, and I was not afraid at that moment either.

It took the American Embassy a few days to figure out where I was, and once they did, they began to negotiate my release. While I was locked up, an embassy official contacted my mother in Clarkson, Nebraska, to inform her that I was in jail. My mother gave American officials permission to have an article put in the *Omaha World-Herald* about my incarceration.

I believe part of our government's interest in making my imprisonment public was to put pressure on North Yemen to back off. It was sending a message that the United States was watching and Yemen would be held accountable should anything go amiss with me. My story never really made the national news. I found out later, though, that the Vatican had been apprised about the situation. I am sure Mother Teresa knew all about it as well.

Early in 1982, after ten days in jail, I was suddenly told I was to have my picture taken. That was odd news. It was the first break in the normal schedule since I had been there, and that gave me instant hope that I would be getting out.

Once we left the compound for the photograph to be taken—which was for their records—one of my jailers confirmed to me that I was being released and that I would be leaving the country on the next flight out. I was being deported. The embassy's persistent inquiries with Yemeni authorities as to my whereabouts had finally allowed the American ambassador to arrange my release. It all took several days to get worked out.

I was delighted to be gaining my freedom, but it was not my desire to leave. Being forced out left a bitter taste in my mouth because if I were to have to leave, I would have wanted it to be on my terms, not theirs. But I had no choice in the matter. This was a situation totally out of my hands. My disappointment was something I had to surrender or it would poison me.

With hardly any time to catch my breath or adjust to the news, much less stop back at the City of Light to say my good-byes and to gather my few things, I was unceremoniously driven to the airport. The Yemenis were anxious to be rid of me.

I had a Yemeni soldier with me the entire time. The assistant ambassador met me at the airport. I did not have any money for a ticket, but he made sure the American government footed the bill. We went to the exit lounge where he told me the ambassador was concerned that Yemeni security would pretend I was leaving the country and would actually put me back in jail when no one was looking.

Apparently an American had been jailed a month or so prior to my experience, and he was assured he was being deported. Instead, they went through the motions of taking him to the airport, but it was just a public relations ruse. He never got on a plane because they threw him right back behind bars. That is why the ambassador made sure his assistant was present with me. He was there to see that I did get on the plane and that the plane left with me on it.

At the exit lounge was a couple from Holland I had worked with back in Taiz. They used to come to Mass every Sunday. I made sure I sat right next to them because I figured they could provide another check and balance in the intrigue playing out with my departure. They were going from Sana'a to Cairo to Rome—the same flight I was booked on.

I said to the man, "If I'm not on the plane when it takes off, then when you get to Cairo please contact the American Embassy and tell them Father Ken Vavrina never left Yemen."

Being kicked out of the country, and for nothing mind you, other than blind suspicion, was not the way I imagined myself departing. I was disappointed. I truly believe that if I had been left to do my work in peace, I would still be there because I enjoyed every minute of working with the lepers. There is so much need in a place like Yemen, and while I could help only a few people, I did help them. It was taxing but fulfilling work.

Ultimately, I was on the plane bound for Cairo, and I did make it there without incident. And from there I made it to Rome as planned. However, I was uncomfortable and self-conscious on those flights because I was a smelly mess. In the haste to get me on my way, I really did not have time to clean up well.

We arrived in Rome at about four-thirty in the morning on St. Patrick's Day. It was cold. I found out the buses do not leave the airport until maybe six, so I sat in the airport until then. During my wait, I contacted my mother to let her know I had been released and was safe in Rome. It was highly emotional.

Naturally she had worried and now she was greatly relieved. She had no idea what might happen to me in Yemen because I was totally under their control. They could have done anything they wanted and had no accountability at all. I talked to my brother and to a friend, Pat Wacha (formerly Pat Hefti). Pat is a writer who wrote many articles about me when I was working with lepers and subsequently when I was with Catholic Relief Services. Pat is a freelancer and her work about me appeared in various small-town Nebraska papers as well as in the *Catholic Voice*, the official newspaper of the archdiocese of Omaha.

Catholic Relief Services had a regional office in Rome headed by Monsignor Joseph Harnett. I knew that office because I had been there before I left Rome for Yemen. In the years I had been away working with lepers, Harnett and I communicated via letter. He asked a number of times, "Would you like to work for CRS?" and I kept saying no, explaining that I was happy working with the lepers.

Now that I was back in Rome, I decided I was going to the CRS office straightaway. The trouble was I still stunk like a pig. My cleanup efforts in the airport and on the plane were rather rushed and haphazard. When I showed up at CRS, I surprised them, not only with my appearance, but with my very presence because they had not gotten word of my release from jail. Graciously, CRS immediately arranged for me to stay at a convent.

Less than twenty-four hours from being in jail, only to be let out so I could be expelled, I found myself in Monsignor Harnett's office. Seeing me in my rather miserable state, he asked me the same question he had been asking in our correspondence, "Would you like to work for CRS?" Only this time I said yes. It was the right opportunity at the right time.

This was about a year after a major earthquake in southern Italy, much of it centered in Potenza, where the quake had caused extensive damage. Hearing my response, Monsignor Harnett said, "Fine, you're part of our staff as of now, and after you get up to speed here, we'll put you to work administering the southern Italy earthquake program." Just like that, I had my first job with CRS. I had a lot to learn though.

Catholic Relief Services was founded in 1943 by the Catholic Bishops of the United States to serve World War II survivors in Europe. It has grown to reach almost one hundred million people in ninety-three countries on five continents. Its mission is to assist impoverished and disadvantaged people in need overseas, regardless of their race, religion, or ethnicity.

In accordance with Catholic teachings, CRS respects the sacredness and dignity of all human life. Clearly, it is an organization after my own heart. You just know when something is a good fit, and CRS fit me to a tee because its work focused on meeting the needs of the destitute and displaced. Bringing relief to people like these is what I left my own country to do.

The next day CRS made arrangements for me to have an audience with the Holy Father. It was a nice recognition for my work in Yemen and for having regained my freedom after being jailed.

Thank God I was finally able to clean up properly. After a long hot shower and a shave, I got dressed in a suit and collar. I was still stooped over from all those days in jail, but some stiffness was not going to keep me from an audience with Pope John Paul XXIII.

I arrived at the Vatican, and as I passed through the entrance, a Swiss Guard clicked his heels and saluted me, and I thought to myself, "Boy, what a difference a day makes." I had gone from the drudgery of being a nameless, faceless inmate in jail to the honor of being saluted by a Swiss Guard on my way to receive a blessing from the pope. I had gone from squalid conditions to sublime, palatial trappings. I had gone from being subjected to interrogation and incarceration to being embraced with love and respect.

John Paul received about two hundred or three hundred of us during this by-invitation-only papal audience. The beloved Polish pope was a wonderful man. He had a warm smile and real charisma. Since his passing, there is much support for his being made a saint for all the work he did preserving the faith in the face of Nazis during World War II and then Communists in the Cold War and for helping foster independence in his native Poland.

———|———

After a whirlwind twenty-four hours, I began to settle into my new life and work. CRS has been doing its thing for a long time, and I soon learned it has the systems and protocols and expertise in place to know how to deal with emergencies. It works cooperatively with other organizations such as the International Red Cross.

Many months before I got there, CRS and other NGOs (nongovernmental organizations) had worked with the Italian government to provide immediate relief to the people left homeless and out of work by the earthquake. So by the time I arrived, the most pressing needs of the injured and dispossessed had been responded to, and CRS was then engaged in construction and reconstruction or repair of homes, businesses, and infrastructure.

Because I needed to know CRS from the ground up, I literally started out sweeping the floor and quickly worked my way up. Then I felt confident to assume the directorship of the CRS program for southern Italy. I ramped things up there. As I recall, we had a $26 million program in southern Italy. I think a portion of those funds came from a group of Italian-Americans who contributed significantly to the relief effort. Most Italians in the United States are from southern Italy or Sicily, and they were generous with their giving.

Monsignor Harnett was a dream boss. The Philadelphia native was a great man. He had been with Catholic Relief Services for decades. He had been everywhere, done everything. Smart as a whip. I was fortunate to know him and to have him befriend me because he was probably the most influential person in the CRS world at that time. His influence is why I got into CRS just like that.

The areas damaged by the natural disaster have a long history with quakes. I worked in Italy two years, at first based in Rome and then in Salerno, which was right next to the earthquake zone.

Another reason I adapted well to CRS is that it is all about getting on with its work and not getting distracted by side issues. For example, it does not proselytize. As their motto says, "Need not creed." Most of its workers are lay people and non-Catholics. They do relief work but much of their focus is on empowering poor people to take care of themselves self-sufficiently. It is a great organization, and for every dollar donated to CRS, ninety-two cents goes to assist the poor in developing nations.

There was much work to do in Italy, but I also had ample time to enjoy the fruits of what the Italians call La Dolce Vita or the Sweet Life. Oh, I loved Italy. It is a most beautiful country. I was in Salerno and Naples most of my time there. The ocean, the architecture, the art, the food, the wine, and the people are just wonderful. I was in southern Italy and the southern Italians have good hearts. They live a rustic, rural but ever-so-rich life.

What a change from working with lepers in an arid land ruled by harsh laws. Where my last hosts had accused me of things I didn't do, threw me in jail and then deported me, the Italians literally embraced me with open arms. It was like day and night.

When the Italian program was wrapping up in 1985, CRS asked me if I would like to work in Juba, the capital city in southern Sudan. South Sudan has been in conflict for decades. I agreed to go, and I was about one week away from leaving—I had all my documentation, my briefing papers, my airline ticket—when an American was shot dead in Khartoum.

CRS put a halt to my going, saying, "No, we're not going to send another American to Sudan at this time." That is when they came back to me and asked if I would like to go to India. Always the faithful servant, I said, "Sure…fine. When do I leave?"

I was given briefing papers for India, but it was all a rather quick turnaround, so I did not have a chance to be schooled in as much depth as I would have liked. That's been the story of my life abroad. India made it mandatory to have a visa and a work permit to be there legally. India was strict at that time about foreigners coming into the country because of the labor situation. They did not want foreigners to come in and take jobs away from Indians, which is why I had to have an explicit reason to be there and to work there.

Those things aside, I looked at the new assignment in India as another bridge to cross, another adventure to experience. I was eager for the opportunity of being introduced to a new culture and a new set of challenges.

INDIA:

With Mother Teresa

I found myself in India where virtually everybody we served was hungry. We used food as a "come on" to get mothers to bring their babies in for monitoring and shots.

My new position was director of the Catholic Relief Services program in Cochin in the Southern India state of Kerala. Cochin is a major port city on the west coast of India by the Arabian Sea. Kerala is the most Christian and the most Catholic of all the states in India, which means the people are on average better educated, the women especially, than in other states. The more education the woman has, the higher the standard of living because she has fewer children and she can take better care of her children. What a contrast to where I was to end up in India.

I arrived in India in 1986. I was in Cochin for nine months, and then I spent the rest of my six years in India in Calcutta.

While in Cochin, I was in charge of CRS development efforts for the southwest part of India. Our budget was approximately $6 million. I oversaw a staff of a few dozen people. This was a comparatively small program to what I would oversee in Calcutta.

We had a lot of food coming in by ship to this seaport. The food was stored in warehouses and transported to where it needed to go by trucks. We were working mainly with mothers and children in the maternal child health programs. We worked with our counterparts in the Indian community to help get the mothers to come in for food. Virtually everybody there is hungry, after all.

The mothers would invariably bring their babies with them, and then staff would use that opportunity to record the child's weight and height to see if they were developing properly. Babies would be given the required shots. In the bargain, the mothers got food to take home. We worked with maybe half a million mothers in the maternal child health program in this way in and around Cochin.

By contrast, in Calcutta, where the population is many times greater, we worked with millions of mothers. I mean, this is India. So many people live there that it defies imagination.

The food was also given out in exchange for work. The monsoons there disrupt vital food production such as the rice harvest. If there is not going to be a rice harvest, then that means people starve.

In villages where there was sloping land, we would enlist the people to construct a dam to hold back the monsoon rains. Not only would they receive food for their labor, but they would have constructed something that protected their future food harvests. With a dam in place, the monsoon rains would come, but instead of washing away, the water would go into the ground. That made it possible for villages to have two rice crops instead of one. That made a big difference in human hunger.

As with my previous stops, I learned quickly the ways things were done in India. I always found I needed to understand the milieu in which I was working. I needed to know what I could do and could not do as an American in India or Yemen or, later, in Liberia and Cuba, just as I had to understand what I could and could not do as an outsider coming into North Omaha or onto the reservation.

Absent that sensitivity and grasp for how personal, social, and business affairs are conducted, I could not effectively do my work. It is all about building trust with the people and demonstrating to them that I care enough to learn these rules of the road. That is particularly vital in work overseas. Cultural competency is a must for the savvy and schooled visitor—no matter the venue.

Like in Yemen, India is also strict with its cultural practices and prohibitions. Fortunately, CRS already had a long history in India, and I quickly brought myself up to speed by studying the briefing papers and files on hand. In that sense it was not as if I was stepping into something brand new. The existing procedures and relationships gave me a framework and guide to work within.

In a place like Cochin, which is a major seaport, getting the food delivered to the port by ship was the easy part. We had warehouses and trucks. We had a whole apparatus and infrastructure. The hard part was then getting the food into the hands of the people who needed it. That is the biggest challenge in any developing nation.

What makes food distribution in these scenarios a problem is corruption. Corruption is always the biggest challenge. It is understandable, too, because these are poor countries with millions of hungry people. When hundreds or thousands of tons of food are introduced into a desperate situation like that, the temptation to steal or divert or make money from it is great. One reason CRS sent me to Cochin was that corruption there was rife. My bosses wanted me to go in there to clean things up. It was like being the new sheriff in town and laying down the law.

Sad to say, one of the worst offenders and exploiters of the system was a fellow priest, Father Thomas. The locals called him Barefoot Father Tom because all the time he was in India he never wore shoes. He was corrupt as can be. He was putting money in his pocket. We got him off the program pronto.

CRS obtained its food from the United Nations World Food Program. There was an agreement that the food provided to us for distribution could not be monetized or sold. We were held accountable. To try and prevent any funny business from happening, we worked closely with our counterparts in the field. We had contracts with food-for-work participants. In exchange for an individual or organization building something—like the dams—CRS would provide so many pounds of rice.

We had monitors to check to see that the contracts were not violated. There was a lot of oversight. Even our best efforts did not always work. Though we closely tracked the food to ensure it was not being held back or doled out to special interests in exchange for money, it sometimes ended up in the wrong hands or was held hostage. Food was like gold and anyone brazen enough to make money from it could line their own pockets. Greed and opportunity cause people to do terrible things.

I am not one to brag, but I am a good administrator. I never procrastinate. I think that is the key to being a good administrator. That, and knowing what you have to do and being tough enough to do it. You have to be tough. Maybe part of it is inherited because my brother is a smart businessman and so was our uncle.

When the administrator of the CRS program in Calcutta became seriously ill, I was tapped to replace him. What awaited me in Calcutta, where I had never been before, nothing could have prepared me for.

———•———

I will never forget my first night in Calcutta. After my flight from Cochin landed, I hailed a taxi to take me to my hotel. It was dark. The weak illumination from the headlights of the taxi and surrounding vehicles along with the glow from irregular street lamps and businesses still open revealed a series of strange shapes as we motored on.

I kept noticing all these sacks alongside the road, and I said to the driver, "What are in these sacks we keep passing by? Is it food? Are these bags of potatoes or rice? Or maybe garbage?"

And he turned around and said, "Those are people." Hundreds upon thousands of people made their beds and homes alongside the road. It was a scale of homelessness I could not fathom. That was my introduction to Calcutta.

Even though I had worked with lepers in Yemen and lived in a dirt-floor hut for five years, I was scared of Calcutta. Of the push and pull and crunch of the staggering numbers of people. Of the absurd overcrowding in the neighborhoods and

Father Ken meets
with Mother Teresa in
Calcutta where he took
his lead from her to serve
the poorest of the poor.

streets. Of the overwhelming, mind-numbing, heartbreaking, soul-hurting poverty. That mass of needy humanity makes for a powerful, sobering, jarring reality that assaults all the senses. That is Calcutta.

I put in long hours in the office, and that meant I would go home in the dark. Being close to the equator, it gets dark early, so you don't have the long evenings like you have in America. Almost every evening coming home from the office, I would drive around one certain corner and see the same young mother with her four children, bathing them on the street. So many live on the street. There is no welfare or Medicaid, there is no safety net, no nothing at all except for what people can scrounge and beg. That is why people starve.

It is really impossible to describe the streets of Calcutta, where only God knows the true size of the population. A place like that must be experienced in the flesh to really know it. *The City of Joy* by Dominique Lapierre is a book that does a good job of painting the picture of what it is like.

I often say to religious and lay people alike, "Go to Calcutta and walk the streets for six days and it will change your life forever." Walk the streets there for one day and even one hour, and it will change you. I know it did me.

You cannot conceive of how the poorest of the poor get by until you are there on the ground with them and can observe it firsthand with your own eyes. There are so many people living in abject poverty and hunger, but the only way you can understand the dimensions of it and what their day-to-day existence looks like is to be there.

You also cannot know unless you experience it is that despite or perhaps because of their lack of material things, these incredibly poor people are generally happy. They have a humility and gratitude and serenity that is a model for us all. Their hand-to-mouth life is hard and can be cruel, but the simplicity of it removes all extraneous expectations. The need to put some food on the table each day is their paramount concern. The women are all pencil thin because they eat less. By custom, the husband eats first, then the children eat next, and whatever is left over the mother eats. Those women are saints, absolute saints.

Food is the most precious commodity there. It is always a scarce resource in great demand, and because there is never quite enough to go around, everyone is "on the make" to get what they can. It is like that wherever poverty and hunger exist.

I once told a reporter, "Things are so bad in the ghettos that children steal the garbage from my hands before I can throw it away." That is not an exaggeration. If food would be thrown away that was still edible, it would be eaten by someone. I learned that you will eat anything if you are hungry enough. I told that same reporter that "starvation is seeing a little boy drink his own urine." Because of the shortage of clean water, people would drink their own urine for the hydration and the nourishment it provided. I came to learn that starvation is mothers who have no milk. Starvation is little babies with wizened, old faces and distended stomachs. They are the faces of poverty.

Pope Francis refers to the poor as powerless, and it is the powerless who starve and suffer. The Church and the government and the corporate sector are powerful. Until there is a redistribution of wealth in the world so that everyone has equal access to the same resources, it will be the responsibility of the powerful to make up the difference for the powerless.

In many cases the powerless lack not only material and physical needs but information and education to help lift themselves out of poverty. When the abdomens of babies swell, mothers in developing nations mistakenly believe their babies are doing well when in fact they are severely malnourished. Once in a malnourished state, the child retains all this fluid and then dies.

Part of development work is giving the poor the resources they need to be self-sufficient, to be informed, to be educated. So much suffering could be alleviated simply by giving poor people these basic human rights, but too often they do not get what they need.

After witnessing these realities, I gained a new appreciation for life and for what I have. I say to myself, "Never complain about anything," not when I saw children and mothers dying of starvation.

In my experience, men have it much easier than women in those desperate conditions. Men can always take care of themselves. They can get a gun and when you have a gun, you can get anything—sex, money, food. But women are the ones who are with their babies, and they are the ones who get sick and die. And little children, when there is nothing in the mother's breast for them, they die.

My work required me to be in the office Monday through Friday, but it also required me to get out and about to where the people lived and struggled. One weekend I would go into the field to check on the status or progress of new and existing projects. Another weekend I would work with the poor in Calcutta, often with Mother Teresa's sisters. I would bring supplies to these starving mothers wracked with illness and infection.

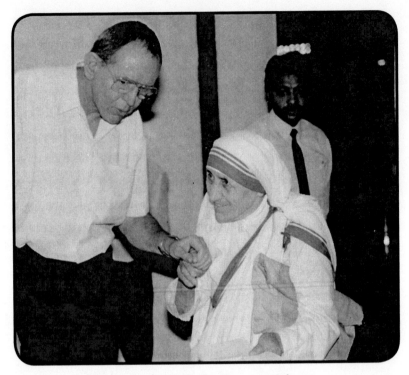

Father Ken with Mother Teresa in Calcutta.

Time and time again I saw profound acts of charity play out. I would bring half a bag of rice to a woman who had nothing to eat for herself or for her children, yet she would take some of that rice and share it with her neighbors. She knew when her neighbors were able to they would share what they had with her. What wonderful people. What wonderful generosity. These are the saints among us. So big hearted. God bless them.

Coming back to the States on vacation from a place like that was difficult because virtually nobody knew anything about Calcutta. I would come back home after being in that other world and find that Americans had no concept of poverty or starvation. People's naïveté, ignorance, and obliviousness to what is happening in the world proved a real challenge for me. That is why coming home to the plenty and comfort of America was always more difficult than going back to the constraints and struggles of the Third World. Ironic, isn't it?

If I were to try to explain what true poverty means I would say it is that the poorest of the poor have no hope for the future. In places like Calcutta, there are no or at best very few opportunities for millions of people to lift themselves out of those conditions for a brighter future.

Orphaned or abandoned street children abound, totally fending for themselves, without parents or guardians for support, with no stable shelter or home to call their own. It is a survival of the fittest existence that pits child against child and even child against adult for what meager scraps can be begged or salvaged and for what outside resources are brought in by aid agencies.

Just as there are countless children on the streets, so too there are untold numbers of adults living in the streets, competing for the same scarcity. We had millions of people in the winter time flood into the already overcrowded city from the neighboring states, especially from tribal areas, in search of work for food. That was their means of surviving. They did not make a single penny for their labor. They would work in the paddy fields and get paid in rice.

When the rice harvest was finished, the man of the family had to find another job. That's why endless streams of them would go into Calcutta and pull rickshaws in order to try and eke out a living. But there are only so many rickshaws to go around, and many would wind up begging on the streets. A lucky man would get one of these big heavy carts on two wheels and push it for three, four, five miles or more through the teeming streets of Calcutta for pennies on the mile. It was cheaper to get men to push a cart by hand than it was to rent a truck. These guys became beasts of burden.

Sometimes they would send some money home to their families, but often they would just drink it away. Mother Teresa understood that and passed no judgment. She never chastised them. She was never tough with the people in that way and perhaps she was forgiving to a fault.

There was a particular rickshaw puller who was a good friend of mine, and sometimes he would let me pull his rig. I just wanted to experience what pulling a rickshaw was like. I am a free spirit that way. There I was, a tall, skinny white guy pulling a rickshaw in the middle of Calcutta. Can you imagine? As I came to find out, pulling is easy, stopping is what's hard. You have to be careful because of the congestion of people and cars and bicycles on the street.

The thing that was endearing about Calcutta is that I could be standing next to the prime minister or an important person just as easily as I could a homeless person. I would not necessarily know the distinction because most of the monied or high-status people there are not ostentatious. They live rather simply too. Another thing I liked about Calcutta is that the women in some parts of that sprawling city and the surrounding rural areas enjoy a degree of freedom that most women there do not have. The women in Calcutta, for example, are encouraged to rise up.

Farther north in India where there is more Hindu influence and elsewhere where the caste system is stronger, women improving or advancing themselves in this way is discouraged or forbidden. Whenever women have a chance to rise and to become empowered, the community thrives. As I like to say, "When you help a mother, you help a village."

Too many women are stuck in lives that offer little hope for breaking the bonds of poverty and custom. I tear up easily, and I did a lot of crying in Calcutta seeing people's potential nullified. What got me through the tough days and the tough times was seeing the good that people were doing and seeing the spirit of giving in people.

It was heartbreaking to see mothers under those terrible conditions raising their children and doing what they had to do for survival. If it meant punching a hole in an open water line to get water to bathe in or to cook with or to drink, they did it. Everything we take for granted here is done with such difficulty there. Their daily survival is done with such difficulty and yet with such grace.

It happened every time we would take food to people that the mothers receiving the rations would share it with other mothers. They were all in this together. Each mother realized her own children and the other mothers' children were one big family dependent on each other for survival, and so they would share everything and they were happy to freely give and so grateful to humbly receive.

It was wonderful to see such goodness expressed in such a loving way. It was such a contrast to the often self-centered and spoiled lives we lead in America, where materialism can trump charity. It reinforced my faith in the basic goodness of people and in the enormous fortitude of people and their will to survive. Even the suffering have the capacity to be kind and, more often than not, they are.

I am not naïve. I am not saying that all of the people I met in developing nations were saints. The shrewd and the crooked took advantage of people. Predators preyed on the weak and the defenseless. But the simplicity of life and particularly the simplicity of the poorest of the poor was endearing, inspiring, refreshing.

In the West we are burdened by our attachments to things. Free of the attachments that bog many of us down in the trap of accumulating things, the poor are often able to more purely connect with the heart and soul and spirit. Unhindered by attachments, one's path can more directly follow that of Christ's. It is why many people on a spiritual path, regardless of their income or status, release themselves from their attachments.

By stripping away all those things that become obstacles to serenity, we simplify our life and open our heart to the things that really matter. It is what I have done in my own life, and I am so happy to be set free in that way. Simplifying my life helps me to better focus on my true calling, which is being there for others and their needs. Giving rather than receiving is where it is at.

Our office in Calcutta administered a $38 million annual budget for East India, Bangladesh, and Nepal. This is where the poorest of the poor reside, and I was in charge of that area for CRS. We were mainly doing development work. Development work is helping the people "to fish" or to fend for themselves. It is personal empowerment and enterprise development done with one person, one family, one village at a time. Opportunities like the micro-loan-focused Grameen Bank and many other development programs helped elevate and empower the people to be able to help themselves.

Looking back at all my experiences during nineteen years overseas, the strongest and fondest memory is of looking into the eyes of a woman who never had the opportunity to have any control over her life or her children's lives and seeing her have hope for the first time. That happened over and over again to women participating in the Grameen banking system.

Women receiving micro loans to sell food stuffs or crafts were, for the first time, able to generate some income and self-determination for their families. I saw that repeated over and over. Those women were never again the same. I looked into the eyes of those women and they were completely changed. They had hope and confidence where there was none before.

Grameen Bank is an international micro-finance organization and community development bank. First implemented in Bangladesh, the program makes small loans to the poor without requiring collateral. Founder Muhammad Yunus, an educator, launched it as a research project to study the possibility of designing a credit delivery system to provide banking services for the rural poor who could not otherwise qualify for loans or credit.

As a test, he made a small loan to a group of forty-two families devastated by famine so they could create small items for sale. When that proved successful, he became convinced that making such loans available to a wide population would help relieve poverty. The idea and the practice quickly caught on and spread throughout India and neighboring nations. It is now a worldwide movement that describes its mission as "connecting the world's poor to their potential." Grameen and Yunus were awarded the Nobel Peace Prize in 2006.

CRS was a major supporter of what has come to be called the Grameen Foundation and invested millions of dollars in Grameen banks. We would go through our counterparts into a village and meet with maybe a dozen women and say, "Would you like to start a business?" Before they could participate in the loan program, they had to demonstrate they could save money. In the next month they would have to save two rupees, which works out to about sixteen cents.

Because these were very capable, motivated women, they would save that sixteen cents and then they would be asked, "If you were given three hundred rupees (which at that time was twenty-four dollars), what would you do with it? Would you start a business? What business would you start?"

The answers would be on the order of, "Well, I could go to the sea and buy fish from the fisherman and go house to house to sell them." Or "I will grow some vegetables and sell them at the market." Or they might make some metal craft or fabric piece to sell to shopkeepers or tourists.

In order to get three hundred rupees, they had to pay 20 percent interest. If they did not pay back the interest and principal in three months, then the program would not be offered to others in their community. In such a communal society as India, this made the loan recipients even more determined to succeed. It was almost one hundred percent certain that these women returned the principal and interest because they wanted their relatives and neighbors and community to benefit from the program as well. It was a rising-tide-lifts-all mentality. This was the beginning of these women going from a subsistence life to a self-sustaining entrepreneurial life.

It is a program that almost exclusively targets women. Why? Men in similar straits are not as likely to return the principal and interest as women are. In my experience it is almost pointless to help a man in these circumstances. The man often does not help his family at all. He drinks or squanders away whatever money he gets and does some crazy, selfish things.

The women are more responsible because they are the primary caretakers. If you help the mothers, you help the family and the children and the community around them. If you help a mother, you help a village. If you help a group of mothers from the same village, you lift that village to a new reality of self-determination.

Grameen was the single most impactful program I saw in action in all of my travels. It truly is teaching people to fish.

When you are the director of CRS Calcutta and you are given $38 million a year and they say, "Ken, you use the money as you think it can be used best," and I get to go ahead and invest in a good thing like the Grameen Bank, that is a gratifying job. What a blessing.

INDIA:

---◆---

12

"God only sees the love in our hearts."

In all my time in India, Mother Teresa was a guiding presence there, whether she was physically present or not.

When I was in Calcutta, there was a conference of about fifty big-time theologians representing different religious denominations discussing how they could work better collegially in the spirit of promoting positive interfaith relations. On the fifth day, they asked Mother to address them.

Mother was not well. She had malaria and arthritis. She was severely bent over and had a hard time walking without assistance. They had to help her up the steps to the stage and to the podium. When she was standing at the microphone, I thought to myself, *What in the world is that woman going to say to this group of PhDs who are convinced that their religion is the true religion and that their liturgy is the best liturgy?*

These men had uttered thousands and thousands of words on top of the many thousands more they had written. And in her magnificent simplicity, Mother looked out on this august body of learned men and only said eight words: "God only sees the love in our hearts."

As the last word left her tongue, I could tell she was going to continue talking but that she had realized in that very moment that she had already nailed it with her short but telling statement, and so without any explanation or ado, she said nothing else and left the stage just as agonizingly as she had arrived.

I had heard her say that same phrase a hundred times, but there in that setting, before that particular audience, it never sounded more profound or sublime.

Mother Teresa addresses a gathering of clergy in Calcutta with Catholic Relief Services. Seated at the table (left to right) are the archbishop of Calcutta, Father Ken, and two representatives from the headquarters of the Catholic Relief Services in Baltimore.

As a wise woman destined for sainthood and in touch with God, she said many things that spoke to truths we all need to hear and practice. Just a few of her famous quotes or reflections on life are among my favorites:

"A life not lived for others is not a life."

"God doesn't require us to succeed;
He only requires that you try."

"I alone cannot change the world, but I can cast a stone
across the waters to create many ripples."

"If we have no peace, it is because we have forgotten
that we belong to each other."

"If we pray, we will believe; if we believe, we will love;
if we love, we will serve."

"If you are humble, nothing will touch you, neither praise
nor disgrace, because you know what you are."

"If you judge people, you have no time to
love them."

"Live simply so others may simply live."

"The good you do today may be forgotten tomorrow.
Do good anyway."

"When you don't have anything, then you
have everything."

"Yesterday is gone. Tomorrow has not yet come.
We have only today. Let us begin."

"Being unwanted, unloved, uncared for, forgotten by everybody, I think that is a much greater hunger, a much greater poverty than the person who has nothing to eat."

"I have found the paradox, that if you love until it hurts, there can be no more hurt, only more love."

"If you can't feed a hundred people, then just feed one."

"It is a kingly act to assist the fallen."

"Love is a fruit in season at all times, and within reach of every hand."

"One of the greatest diseases is to be nobody to anybody."

"We cannot do great things on this Earth, only small things with great love."

And my favorite: When asked why she embraced a leper, Mother said, "Because he is my Lord." Not many people heard her say this because she and I were giving a tour of the City of Light to some UN officials. Mother showed them how we tend to the lepers, and when she embraced one particularly afflicted woman, the UN official visibly gasped. Then she asked Mother why. This was Mother's response.

Her collected observations and affirmations are a call to love and to service. They form a kind of catechism for how to live a life of meaning and wholeness. I needed her advice as much as the next person. So often she would say to me, "Oh, Father Ken, you need to become more transparent." She knew that I liked to have all my ducks lined up all in a row like a typical tightly wound American, and she was letting me know that I should surrender and let God work through me. She was telling me, "Don't do things the way you want to do them, rather let God do things through you as He wants them done." It is good advice. Thy will, not mine, be done.

Mother Teresa was already a world-famous figure by the time I arrived in India and that meant spiritual travelers made their way to her Mother House and to the House of the Dying that her sisters operated. I celebrated well over a hundred Masses in the Mother House in Calcutta, and having Mass there was a real challenge because most of the time there was no reliable electricity. She did not have a generator either.

The altar was by the open windows, and right outside was a busy road with rattling trolley cars running both ways, so I had to just about shout at the top of my voice to even be heard over all the noise. Mass was held in the chapel, and there were maybe fifty nuns and fifty volunteers there on average.

I was having Mass at the Mother House in Calcutta one day, and I looked out and the Governor of California, Jerry Brown, was there. I recognized him right away, and afterward I went to speak with him. He had ended up in Calcutta, as many do, as part of a personal spiritual journey and call to be of service. He was working in the Home for the Dying as a volunteer and living in a poor hotel. He wanted to maintain a low profile and remain incognito at all costs. This was clearly no photo op for him.

He earnestly said to me, "Don't tell anybody I'm here." I respected his privacy and did as he asked. Until now.

Mother was tough with her sisters. She never permitted them to go out and eat with anybody outside of the order because she assumed they would be inclined to dine with the richer people rather than the poorer people. So her sisters stayed in the convent to take their meals. I suppose part of the rationale behind that, too, was for her sisters to prove their commitment and obedience. She expected the sisters to live in poverty, and that they did.

They had nothing in the way of personal possessions. They slept on the floor and lived as the poor people they served did. In fact, the Missionaries of Charity lived Mother Teresa's life. Each sister just had two saris—one they wore and one they washed. They traveled with a little canvas satchel over their shoulder that contained everything they owned.

They followed a rigid routine. The sisters would get up at five in the morning and pray. Then came chores—they would clean up the convent and do their laundry. Mass would be at seven. After Mass the sisters would have breakfast and then go into various areas of the city to do their work alongside volunteers. This was their schedule. Sometimes Mother went with her sisters, but most times she did not. The sisters would come back at midafternoon to have lunch and take a nap. Then they would take recreation and dinner and go to bed by eight.

If her sisters did not already have the fear of God in them, then Mother made sure to put it in them. She made sure they were afraid of her too. I saw her pushing sisters around, figuratively speaking. She was very domineering. When she would travel to her sisters' communities, she would immediately run roughshod over everyone.

I remember one time she came to visit one of her Sisters of Charity centers where there was a large orphanage and school. The sisters had a lot of laundry to do there, and they did it all by hand. The only device they had to assist in the washing was a hand-cranked wringer to wring the water out. When Mother caught sight of it, she ordered the sisters to "get rid of it." Even that simple contraption was too much for them to have in her eyes. And the sisters did as they were told without delay.

That kind of autocratic approach does not work with everyone. More and more of her sisters were coming from Europe and the Americas and even from more affluent areas in India, and they brought with them more progressive ideas. They wanted to have a few things she forbade and they wanted to do development work. They wanted to teach the people how to fish—to be self-sufficient—rather than just minister to their spiritual needs and maybe give them some food and water.

But Mother said, "No, we're not going to do that, because if the people are able to fish, then they're not the people we need to work with. We're going to work with the people who are hopeless, who cannot learn to fish."

Well, this caused a great deal of consternation in the ranks. She lost a lot of sisters over that because, the way they saw it and the way a lot of others saw it, by not teaching people to be self-sufficient, they were making them dependent on charity and reinforcing their hopelessness, Even so, she would not budge. She was intent on doing things her way.

I disagreed with Mother and I told her so. I knew the value of development work. Our CRS programs in India were proof of its effectiveness. Because I was a priest and she had great respect for priests, she listened to me, not necessarily agreeing with me at all. She just politely listened and then went right ahead and did her own thing anyway. Stubborn. I may have disagreed with her and some of her methods, but I supported her.

I remember my last Mass in the Mother House coincided with the "revolt" happening within her community. CRS headquarters had asked me if I would be willing to become the director of the Liberia, Africa, program, and I agreed. Before leaving for Liberia, I came to the Mother House to find all this turmoil taking place with some sisters wanting to leave to do development and to have a few things that Mother said they could not have. In such a contentious climate, I wished to offer a symbol of harmony and autonomy, so I used the image of a leaf.

I said, "My prayer is that the Missionaries of Charity be like a leaf floating in the wind to permit the Holy Spirit to move them in whatever direction it has them to move. To let the spirit guide them in their work." That was my final message to share. Mother was present and she appreciated that.

I cried the day I left Calcutta in 1991. I loved Calcutta. Mother Teresa had tears in her eyes as well. We had become very good friends. She was the real deal. She was hands on, and she was not afraid to get her hands dirty. She was a physical person. She would touch me the way a friend touches me. I once told a reporter that being around her was comfortable, adding, "It was like being with your own mother—you knew you were accepted."

Yes, she truly accepted and loved unconditionally. She did a lot of traveling to be out among the people. One of her favorite expressions was, "I've got to run," and off she would go to this meeting or that meeting. She was always busy, always going someplace, always active. She was full of energy and just absolutely tireless in her work. I used to tell her she had ants in her pants and she would laugh. She laughed at my stories and my jokes. She loved to laugh. She laughed a lot.

When I would venture out of the office to work on the streets of Calcutta, I would often accompany some of her sisters and sometimes I would go out with Mother herself. I saw her on many occasions kneeing on the filthy sidewalk working with somebody who was dying, her sari stained with that person's feces and blood. It would not bother her at all. She and her sisters and the volunteers who worked alongside them helped these people to continue to live on the streets or transported them to one of Mother's homes or to a hospital.

I certainly admired how she created a vocation to serve the poorest of the poor within her larger vocation of service. Born in Macedonia, she was originally a member of the Irish order of nuns, the Loreto Sisters of Dublin. Serving in that order is what initially introduced her to Calcutta. She was teaching at an exclusive girls' school there, St. Mary's High School for Girls, run by the Loretos. Its students came from the city's poorest Bengali families.

She learned to speak Bengali and Hindi fluently. She eventually became principal at the school. Her living space was on the second level of an adjacent convent that she and her fellow Loreto sisters stayed in. Looking out from her perch, she could see the poor people on the other side of the walled-in campus. She asked her superior if she might be able to go outside the gate to minister to the people, and the superior gave her permission. Thus, she saw for herself how the people dwelling in the slums lived.

Mother Teresa told me she was on the train to the Himalayan foothills when the task of starting the Missionaries of Charity was given to her. She described how something entered her mind and heart, the way it did with me to enter the priesthood, that she should start a religious order of Indian nuns that would work with the poor and sick and dying. They would especially work with the most vulnerable of all these populations: women and children. And this work would be carried out right in the slums where few outsiders normally ventured.

When she got back, she told the local church hierarchy what she had been called to do. Forming a new order is never easy and almost always meets with skepticism and resistance and, of course, bureaucratic delay. Complicating matters for Mother was the fact she was non-Indian. It took much praying and lobbying by her to get her superiors to see things her way, though she made it clear it was God's way and will she was trying to fulfill, not merely her own. It was only because of her steadfast and tough determination that after many disappointments she was able to get the Church to agree to let her form a new community to do this work.

The archbishop of Calcutta, Ferdinand Périer, gave her his blessing to go out among the great unwashed. She started out with zero. This meager beginning eventually turned into the international Missionaries of Charity. Her order established a hospice and centers for the blind, aged, and disabled, and a leper colony. She was summoned to Rome in 1968, and in 1979 she received the Nobel Peace Prize for her humanitarian work.

The first home she built was Kalighat Home for the Dying, a free hospice for the poor. It was very simple. Dying people for whom nothing could be done to save their life were brought in from the streets to literally die there while being lovingly, compassionately cared for.

I remember one man saying as he was being ministered to on the street, "I lived like a rat and I'm dying like an angel," as Missionaries of Charity cared for him with food and water, touch and prayer. I remember one time I was walking down a street in Calcutta and there was a young boy of maybe seven or eight years of age lying on the sidewalk. He was naked with a crowd of people around him.

Someone next to me was speaking English and said, "What should we do with him?" and someone else said, "Let's take him to Mother Teresa." And another person in the crowd said, "Well, do you think Mother Teresa will accept him?" to which the first person said, "Mother Teresa accepts everybody." And it is true, she did accept everybody without qualification.

Later, I saw that same boy who was the topic of that conversation safely ensconced in one of her homes. You see, Mother didn't tell people what to do. She lived by her example and let people act out of their own conscience and compassion. When people see the right thing in action, they usually do the right thing themselves.

Wherever Mother went and whatever she did, whether walking the city streets or visiting a rural village or giving a public speech or meeting with some bigwigs at some fancy venue, her presence caused a stir the way a rock star or movie star does. Her reputation preceded her, and the warm, adoring, awe-struck reception people gave her expressed their love and admiration for her.

Whenever she came to the CRS office in Calcutta, it was the same way. Frantic workers scurried about saying, "Mother is coming, Mother is coming..." They nearly fell over each other ushering her into my office. She would come to CRS because she needed something—there was a flood someplace or a drought somewhere, and people needed help and we always helped. We worked cooperatively with her and the Missionaries of Charity to get things done.

Indira Gandhi, the former prime minister of India, loved Mother Teresa. She told Mother her sisters could go anywhere they wanted in the country for free. Not a rupee would ever be charged a sister for travel on Indian Airlines.

Calcutta had a communist government, a communist mayor, and Mother got along beautifully with them. She was quite the politician and diplomat when she had to be. During my tenure there, a particularly devastating cyclone hit the region, one especially prone to these natural disasters. I mentioned to Mother that CRS was trying to get supplies into the hardest hit areas in Bangladesh, but we could not get anything out because of the endemic corruption and red tape.

So Mother said to me, "Let's go to Indian Airlines." When we got to the airline's headquarters for the eastern region, we were ushered right up to the office of the director, Mr. Kakkar, and after introducing me to him and explaining what the problem was, she looked him straight in the eye and said, "Give him an airplane, he has to take some rice to these starving people."

He replied, "Mother, I'm sorry, I don't have an airplane to give you," and typical of her she said, "I'm going to give you an opportunity to receive God's blessings. Now don't you have a flight going into Darkar every day?"

He said, "Yes, Mother."

And she continued, "Well, why don't you put food on each of these flights and it will get there for free."

That evening I was in Darkar with many kilograms of food. Her directness and decisiveness combined with her earnest appeal to this man's better nature accomplished what all my complaining and haggling could not.

Mother Teresa had a knack for making things happen. Now the setting was Ethiopia, Africa. I was just a rookie at that time with CRS. There was a crisis and people were starving and our program and her sisters were trying to address the situation. Food was coming in from the United Nations food program. One of the stipulations was that the supplied food could never be sold or bought. Recipients were prohibited from cashing the food in, so to speak, for money and then using the money for the poor.

The Inspector General's office in Washington, DC, was upset that Mother's sisters were not following proper protocols, so that office contacted the US Attorney General's office to have someone fly to Ethiopia to have a face-to-face meeting with her.

I was present at this meeting between an official from the Attorney General's office in his three-piece power suit and Mother in her simple blue and white sari. This attorney was really laying the law down with Mother, trying to intimidate her by saying, "If we find out any of your sisters are not properly monitoring the food, the Missionaries of Charity will not be allowed to assist in this food program."

Truth be told, her sisters never did anything like careful monitoring. They didn't do any administration. They never had a sheet of paper as to who got what. That was just not how they did things.

This attorney droned on, saying, "We need to have accountability for every bag of rice."

There were about ten of us around a conference table, and Mother reached behind her to grab a pencil and she asked, "Does anybody have a piece of paper?"

Right in front of all of us, she wrote out a letter, saying the words aloud as she wrote, "Dear Ronald..."

Dumbfounded, we all realized she was composing a personal letter to her friend, President Ronald Reagan, complaining about what happened at this meeting with this attorney second-guessing, nitpicking, and chastising the methodology of her and her sisters. When she was finished, she signed the letter "M. Teresa."

There was never a problem again with her sisters being called to task for insufficient oversight and lax procedures. That was Mother Teresa. She knew how to get things done, and she was not above using leverage or calling in favors from powerful friends, one of whom just happened to be the leader of the free world.

It was years later, long after having left India for Liberia and having returned to the States that I read to my dismay, as others did, that Mother Teresa had experienced the dark night of the soul and suffered a crisis of faith that persisted through most of her adult life.

I knew her well and yet I never detected any indication, any sign that she was burdened with this internal struggle. Not once in all the time I spent with her did she betray a hint of this. She seemed in all outward appearances to be quite happy and jovial. However, I did know that she was very intense about her faith and her work. In her mind and heart she was never able to do enough. She never felt she did enough to please God, and so there was this constant, gnawing void she felt that she could never fully fill or reconcile.

Quite simply, she didn't think God loved her. It is terrible to imagine she thought that. I mean, as we grow in faith, we should be moving in just the opposite direction. We should be more convinced that God loves us, we should be more faithful, and not thinking that God isn't our loving shepherd. I think the people who go through what she did are the ones who are really intense and very intent on being holy and always doing the right thing. She was driven in her spiritual life. Mother often said, "You can only work with one person at a time." That is what she said, but she didn't practice it.

I do not mean to suggest Mother harbored an inflated view of herself. No, she was humble in all things. All the fame and accolades that came her way had no bearing on her at all. Her appearance meant nothing to her. No face cream had ever touched that leathery skin. She was extremely wrinkled, and she could not have cared less. But I do believe her expectations were out of alignment with her mission of being a reflection of God's love, mercy, grace, and healing power in each person she met and that her work touched. She truly believed that when she was ministering to the poor, she was ministering to God.

Reality, though, dictated that she could only reach so many people at any given time, and her feeling that God had somehow abandoned or forsaken or neglected her because she could not get to them all was her ego getting in the way. The ego is what gets any of us in trouble. The more we can suppress it or better yet surrender it to God's will, the better off we will be. When we put our ego aside to be in alignment or agreement with God's will is when we find true contentment and serenity. Let go and let God.

Now that she is gone, what I miss most about her is her friendship and her sanctity really—the example she gave me of prayer, of dedication, of one hundred percent commitment.

She almost literally never took time for herself, and surely this extreme workaholism was to the detriment of her emotional and physical health. She was always doing something for others, always. She would make her way to a Missionaries of Charity center or home early in the morning, and she would still be meeting with the sisters until late at night. I don't know when she slept but that was just how she drove herself day after day, always pressing forward, always striving to do the next right thing.

My experience in India is never far from my thoughts. It expanded my world view and at the same time it gave me a deeper, more personal understanding of the human condition. It confirmed for me that if we strip away all the external things—title, position, income, living accommodations, possessions—we are all the same.

Our struggles and successes may look different on the outside, but we are all striving to do the best we can with what we are given. We are all called to do the right thing. No matter what our circumstances, we can be a reflection of God's light and love. I saw destitute people in India be just that—living examples of light and love through their joy and generosity. They were poor in terms of material possessions, but they were rich in terms of their humanity.

I really did cry when it came time to leave India. I really did not want to leave Calcutta. I truly loved it there. But Catholic Relief Services needed me in Africa, where an entirely different scenario awaited. An on-again, off-again civil war in Liberia had already raged for some time, and now that there was a cessation in hostilities, CRS wanted to start development work there to repair the damage that had been done and to feed the people who had fled their villages.

CRS tasked me with the job because of the development track record of our office in India. So with a reluctant yet expectant heart, I accepted this role. Just as before when leaving one land for another, when going from one assignment to the next, I put my trust in God and crossed the bridge in front of me.

LIBERIA:

13

Civil War, Warlords, and Lawlessness

Reading about a civil war and living through it are two different things. In preparation for my new post in Liberia, Catholic Relief Services provided background information to get me up to speed about this unfamiliar country I would be entering. I did my homework at the end of my tenure in India. The CRS briefs or reports about Liberia were quite enlightening. I learned the country has a fascinating history with a strong American connection.

CRS had been in Liberia for decades, and the assembled staff in our Monrovia headquarters was quite knowledgeable about that country's history, culture, and politics. They helped me understand what led up to the recent war, what conditions were like throughout the nation, and what needs and challenges the population faced.

As I found wherever I went abroad, I depended heavily on my coworkers and staff. We work as a team and eventually become a family. My staff in Liberia was absolutely first-rate with the regular briefings they gave me. Staying current was vital in such a fluid situation, where things could change overnight with these unpredictable warlords and their undisciplined armies. In order to get food and medicine to where it was needed, we had to have accurate, up-to-date information about who the warlords and their field generals were, what areas they controlled, and how best to negotiate with them. We had to know the actors or players at any given moment.

If I was going to be an effective administrator in a foreign land, I not only had to know the lay of the land and the hierarchy of the leadership, but I needed to know something about the character of the nation and its people. That is where steeping myself in the history was useful.

In the case of Liberia, its entire history is associated with unrest and turmoil and factional conflict, so it should be no surprise that its people are divided among the victors and the vanquished, the ruling class and rebels. But in truth the vast majority of its people are steadfast, good-hearted folks who have the capacity to endure.

Well before blacks gained their freedom in the United States, there was support for the establishment of a colony or settlement of blacks from America in Africa because many believed that, whether slave or free, blacks would never be accepted or fully integrated in the United States. That kind of thinking is what led a group of white Americans, many of them slaveholders, to band together under the American Colonization Society to found Liberia.

In the first quarter of the nineteenth century, the ACS established the new colony on a tract of land in West Africa purchased from local tribes. The hope was that freed slaves would move there and their descendants would remain there. Many notable supporters of this endeavor advocated for it in speeches and articles. The ACS encouraged slaveholders to offer freedom to their slaves on the condition that, once emancipated, they would move to Liberia at the society's expense.

The first settlers relocated to Liberia in the 1820s or so. The blatant colonization drew criticism from blacks and from white abolitionists who saw it for what it was—an attempt to rid the United States of African-Americans—and from slaveholders who saw it as a threat to their way of life.

But even outside the ranks of the ACS, colonization had its supporters, particularly the state of Maryland. By the 1840s, the freed slaves who settled in Liberia were struggling under the yoke of hostile local tribes, bad management, and life-threatening diseases. The US government would not claim sovereignty over the colony, thus in 1846 the ACS demanded Liberians declare their independence. By that time thousands of migrants had sailed to Liberia and settled there.

For most of its history, Liberia was dominated by the small minority of black colonists and their offspring, known collectively as America-Liberians. The America-Liberians were an elite class that dominated the indigenous peoples. A strict social-racial caste system isolated the haves from the have-nots and created deep rifts and resentments. Money and education bought the ruling class their power, and for generations they were able to hold onto that power in this master-subservient relationship.

The indigenous populations staged many rebellions to express their discontent. America's loyalties were squarely with the colonists, and the United States even sent naval ships to help quell the unrest. This rank inequality was always destined to result in violence and civil war. Most Americo-Liberians lived privileged lives, untouched by the want and rancor of the lower class. Americo-Liberian customs were heavily influenced by American and British culture, and the ruling class maintained close ties to American stakeholders.

By the second half of the twentieth century, growing economic disparities caused increased hostility between indigenous groups and Americo-Liberians. President William R. Tolbert Jr. suppressed any opposition. When he ordered his troops to fire on protesters holding demonstrations in the streets of Monrovia in 1979, seventy people were killed. Rioting ensued throughout the country, finally leading to a military coup in 1980.

Following a bloody overthrow of the Americo-Liberian leaders by the military, the new regime met resistance, and governmental repression grew. In 1989 tribal and civil war broke out. It was in this dysfunctional milieu that Charles Taylor came to power. He led a Libyan-backed resistance group, the National Patriotic Front of Liberia, that overthrew the Samuel Doe regime that had earlier taken power from Tolbert.

Following Doe's execution, Taylor gained control of a large portion of the country through vicious tactics. He was able to arm his men with weapons he obtained from inside and outside the country because he had access to the diamond fields in northwest Liberia, which financed his war spending. Many of his soldiers raped girls and women. Following a peace deal that ended the war, Taylor intimidated the population into electing him president in the 1997 general election.

When I was there, there was no such thing as an election, Charles Taylor was just the boss. As you will read, I had many dealings with Taylor. After I left, he would be at the center of yet another civil war and eventually be arrested, charged, and convicted of war crimes.

The average Liberian has always been on the wrong side of the divide between whoever was in power and survival. That story has been played out countless times in human history, and I suppose as long as some people are willing to take advantage of other people for their own gain, that unfortunate exploitation will continue.

CRS headquarters in Baltimore sent me there thinking the war was over in Liberia. When I arrived, I did find something like peace and thus the promise that we could indeed do development work there. But I soon learned peace is a relative term and condition in an environment like that where old tribal wounds and antipathies run deep. Just look at the mess in other African nations beset by similar intertribal conflicts or at the competing religious-cultural factions vying for supremacy in the Middle East and in Iraq, Iran, Syria, and Afghanistan.

Violence and war are inevitable consequences whenever one group puts itself above another and forces its will on the other. Once you devalue the humanity of an individual or group, you are one step closer to taking what they have—their home, their land, their livelihood, their way of life. Once you do that, taking someone's life is much easier.

I was in Liberia for no more than two and a half months when the war started up again, and from there it just intensified.

The capital of Monrovia, where our office was located, had been badly destroyed by the war. I would say the city was sixty percent in ruins when I first laid eyes on it. A lot of shelling, grenades, and bombs had wrecked buildings. Some of the population had been dispersed. Conditions worsened with the resumption of war.

Through all that devastation and turmoil, though, the everyday people were compassionate with each other. Yes, the thing that impressed me and that I love about the African people, whom I consider some of the nicest people in the world, is their warm hospitality. During the fighting, families would open their homes to refugees who had fled from the rural areas to come into the city, and suddenly homes of four or five were sheltering twenty or twenty-five people. On their own accord, citizens just went ahead and opened their homes to these strangers. Just wonderful.

Despite all of the problems, all of the dangers, the Liberians remained a joyful people. They obviously knew what was going on. They were not naïve. But they did not let it get them down. The African people have a wonderful, giving spirit. Resilient too. They are bright. The kids really study hard in school, and African adults as a rule are hard working.

When they come to America, they do well for themselves and for their families. I saw this for myself when I returned to the States and became close to the Sudanese refugee population in Omaha. So, you see, I have gleaned these impressions from direct experience with Africans both in their homeland and in America, and this appreciation for them is said by someone who has been around a little bit and seen a few places and interacted with different peoples.

We had a large office in Monrovia—another in a string of port cities I ended up in during my overseas stops. Ships brought in food for us to distribute. We had many warehouses there to store the supplies. We not only had food coming in to help feed the people, we also had development projects going on to help people feed themselves.

Two of my top staffers were fellow Midwesterners. My development director was Krista Riddley. She was a smart, young African-American woman from Des Moines, Iowa, who had a doctorate in international and public affairs from Columbia University. Before working for CRS she worked on Capitol Hill as a legislative assistant. Her CRS career also included stops in Burkina Faso, Gambia, and Niger in various managerial and project-related positions. After Liberia she served as a country representative in Zimbabwe. Today she is a holistic health and wellness coach in the Washington, DC, area.

My agricultural director was Ray Studer, who was from Council Bluffs, Iowa, by way of Kansas. Before joining CRS, he was an Iowa State extension specialist teaching American children the basics of agriculture. A stint in the Peace Corps took him to West Africa and that is what led him to work with CRS in Liberia. He was still there, working in my position, years after I left and weathering the second civil war that Charles Taylor helped ignite.

So there we were, three Midwesterners in a place about as distant and different from our homes as possible.

The CRS program was the biggest yet. I supervised with a $42 million annual budget for mainly delivering food to the hungry and awarding money for community building projects.

There is great potential in Liberia. It has fertile ground and plentiful rain. It could feed all of Africa. One day it is going to be a breadbasket of Africa. But when I was there, they were eating their seed rice and then they had nothing to plant, so we were providing seed rice as well.

We administered a huge program both in terms of scale and responsibility. Administering that size of program in such an unstable political and military climate made everything we did more complicated and dangerous. The war made things even more challenging.

In addition to our main office in Monrovia, we maintained major offices in Buchanan and Harper, which were the other intake and distribution points for the supplies we delivered and the programs we ran. Once the fighting resumed after my arrival, Monrovia and the other cities we had a presence in came under steady attack from rockets and mortars. Fighting went on right outside Monrovia's city limits.

Tension ran high because we were in a section of Monrovia where the war even encroached on us at times. We had one staff member who was killed in Buchanan when one of our warehouses there was attacked. It was a dangerous business. Often, too, we would take convoys into warlord-occupied areas.

I remember several mornings when I would be shaving or brushing my teeth getting ready to go to the office and saying to myself, "I could be killed today," because I was leading a convoy of food into rebel-held territory, and we were at the mercy of these kids with automatic weapons. They would shoot at anybody, they didn't care who you were. They didn't care, for example, that I wore a collar and was a priest and worked for a very large nongovernmental organization. So there was that threat.

I never put another staffer in the lead vehicle in my place. I always took the lead spot. And there were sometimes shots fired. I heard a bullet whistle over my head one time. Wherever we went, there was always the threat of rocket-propelled grenade attacks.

Checkpoints, there were always checkpoints. For example, on the road between Monrovia and Banga, where Charles Taylor had his headquarters, there were between forty or fifty checkpoints set up. In some sectors there were checkpoints every quarter of a mile. And at every one of these checkpoints were young rebel soldiers, kids really, who would stop you and try to get money. They were just totally corrupt. Some of them were high on drugs and alcohol.

These boys cavalierly brandished AK-47s and other guns, and they would sometimes point them at us too. They were not regular soldiers. They had little or no training and discipline. They were either there because they were forced into it or because they were hooked by the thrill of it all. We never knew what was going to happen in those situations with them. Say the wrong thing or look at them the wrong way, and they could kill us just like that, without cause or consequence.

A CRS convoy would consist of three to five trucks filled with food and medicine. Wherever we traveled, we had to deal with the various warlords "in control" of particular areas. There were seven warlords. Charles Taylor was the most powerful, and his forces controlled the most territory; therefore, we had to broker deals with him. The others had to be given their due as well, just not to the same extent. But I had to play a game with all of them—giving them something, even if only respect, in return for safe passage; otherwise, they would just shut us down, make life difficult, and intimidate, harass, or do worse to our convoys and field workers.

This form of extortion was akin to paying tribute to feudal warlords of old or paying protection money to the mob in a more modern context. I could not play favorites, at least not so they could see it, because the warlords were sworn rivals and enemies who often fought each other over contested turf and scarce resources.

The stress and challenge of dealing with that risk and chaos, all to help people in desperate straits, was not for the faint of heart. It was really quite taxing because we had the sense anything could happen at any time in that lawless land. It was guerilla warfare without distinct front lines. The fight was always liable to move, and territories held by one group could fall into the hands of another group overnight and then revert to the first group the following week, and so on.

Warlords had to be dealt with, and they were as changeable as the weather. All of those obstacles and more interfered with the normal flow of resources we were charged with getting to where they were needed. Any delays could be critical because we were providing food to starving people.

Despite the blood Taylor had on his hands, the first thing I needed to do was establish rapport with him because, frankly, he was the most important man in the country.

Our office had a $42-million-dollar annual budget, and we were bringing in a lot of food. The country was at war, and we had to do what we had to do to get the food distributed. Where CRS never allows their country representatives to have anything to do with military people, I decided on my own initiative that I would not be able to do much of anything without establishing a working relationship and partnership with Charles Taylor. I would have been stupid not to work with what I had to work with. Even though his hands were stained with blood, I had to shake his hand and gain his cooperation in order to get anything done. It was a little like dealing with the devil.

I remember well my first meeting with the warlord. It was at his headquarters in Banga, about sixty miles from Monrovia. I had an appointment to see him, yet I had to wait a while for his girlfriends to clear the office. His armed bodyguards and security detail protected the headquarters from assassins. He was an Americo-Liberian because his ancestors came from the United States.

He was rather light complected, and skin tone is part of the lingering caste system that still pervades that land. The tribals, the people who are dark toned, tend to defer to people of lighter color, and those with lighter complexions tend to gravitate to positions of respect and power.

Taylor was a shrewd man, untrusting of everyone. He also had a charisma that drew people to him. Taylor and I hit it off immediately, though, because we understood each other and how we could be of use to one another. He knew I needed him to get the resources to the masses, but he also knew his own soldiers needed some of those same resources to keep them loyal and in line. After all, his soldiers were hungry and sick too, and we had food and medicine to spare.

So sort of under the table, his soldiers got some of the provisions. We just looked the other way and chalked it up as a cost of doing business. In return he enabled us to get into areas where people were starving. He never once denied us access. I always had his ear and cooperation when we needed to respond to a new crisis.

In exchange, his soldiers got what they needed. The fact that his soldiers were not uniformed and thus who could really tell a solider from a nonsoldier helped to keep that arrangement secret. I realized he would not go over my head to get me into trouble with CRS headquarters, who might call the whole thing off, or let word leak out to the other warlords, who might demand the same deal. I knew he would protect me.

And so we played that game well in the five years I was there. We were on friendly terms all that time because we recognized each other as valuable allies. I came to know many of his high-ranking people. I was close with his director of interior. It was vital I kept open channels of communication with Taylor and his bunch. I estimate I communicated with Taylor at least once a week, often via these powerful radios with huge range.

Not for a moment did I ever forget who I was really talking to. Sure, he was my friend when it came to these dealings, but I never forgot that he was a ruthless dictator. He was a pathological liar too. He could look you dead in the eye and tell you an out-and-out untruth, and I swear he was convinced he was telling the truth. A real paranoid egomaniac. But in war you cannot always choose your friends.

Hundreds of thousands of innocent people died in Liberia during those civil wars. There were many atrocities. One in particular touched me personally. On October 20, 1992, five American nuns, all of whom I knew and considered friends, were killed.

I had visited them at their convent two days before this tragedy. They were members of the Adorers of the Blood of Christ. On my visit you could hear the artillery shells and the RPGs exploding in the distance as the rebels moved closer and closer to Monrovia. Because the sisters lived on the outskirts of the city at a compound in the suburb of Gardnersville, they were in a more precarious position relative to the fighting than my own home and office, which were located more in the interior.

I said to the sisters, "You should not be here, it's too dangerous," and it was not that many days afterward that the killings happened. Not all the sisters at the convent were murdered. One I knew well was apprehended, and she was really shaken by the experience and the loss of her friends. She said she and her colleagues stayed despite the approaching danger because they knew these boys who made up the rebel forces. The sisters assumed those ties would protect them from harm, but sadly that proved not the case. The killings were condemned worldwide.

The slain missionaries, all from Illinois, were Sister Barbara Ann Muttra, a nurse who first went to Liberia in 1971; Sister Agnes Mueller, a nurse and teacher; Sister Kathleen McGuire, a teacher; and Sisters Shirley and Mary Joel Kolmer, first cousins and teachers. May they rest in peace.

The war came uncomfortably close on another occasion when I officiated a wedding between one of my American male managers and a Liberian woman during a time when the fighting was escalating and coming to the city. The rumble of rocket fire and bombs punctuated the night. Fighter jets flew overhead. The war really felt near.

The next morning I realized the city was infested with rebels and that got me wondering what happened to our food

in the warehouses at the port. Were our supplies safe or had
they been pillaged? I clambered in my truck and took off to see
for myself. I went as far as I could get when I came to a bridge
I could not cross because thousands of Liberians were fleeing
into the city from the surrounding villages under attack.

I went back to enlist the manager I had just married the
night before to accompany me across the bridge on foot. As we
made our way to the other side, we noted damage to the area
around the port from rockets and artillery, but the warehouses
were intact. All these refugees were coming into the city with
nothing to eat, and we had all the food in the world, so it
became imperative to get the food from the warehouses into
the central part of the city.

I remember this operation clearly. We assembled a fleet of
trucks, and by that afternoon we hauled thirteen truckloads of
food out of the port to where the people were gathered, all the
while the sounds of fighting pressing in around us.

Getting food to the people who needed it came down
to logistics in most cases. CRS had the resources and
connections to procure whatever the situation called for
and often it was hundreds, even thousands, of metric tons of
food. We'd get rice and sorghum in 50-kilo bags. Heavy bags,
but essential life-sustaining food. And medicine. We'd try
to procure malarial drugs and anti-diarrheals and measles
medicine for the children. I could contact headquarters or
one of the neighboring countries, such as Nigeria, to fill
whatever size order was required. We could always get what
we wanted.

Actually putting food in the hands of the hungry people it
was intended for was another matter because of corruption. In

Yemen and India those challenges were manageable compared to what we faced in Liberia, where every obstacle was magnified due to the unstable environment. The danger posed by the war and the greed expressed by the warlords made our job tough.

The instability in Liberia was destabilizing to its West African neighbors. The Economic Community of West African States (ECOWAS) attempted various initiatives aimed at a peaceful settlement. The United Nations supported the efforts of ECOWAS to end the civil war. These efforts included establishing a multilateral armed observer force, the Economic Community of West African States Monitoring Group or ECOMOG. This formal arrangement brought together elements from separate armies, led by Nigerian armed forces, with other units drawn from Guinea, Sierra Leone, Gambia, Liberia, Mali, Burkina Faso, Niger, and others.

There was talk of the American government sending US Marines in as peace-keepers but that would have been disastrous. It was far better to have peace-keepers from the same West Africa region as Liberia than to have them come from the outside. The rebels would have targeted American troops in the same way our troops were targeted in Somalia, and what started as a peace-keeping mission would have turned into a fight. Besides, our troops didn't know the terrain, didn't know the country, didn't know what was going on, and didn't speak the languages. ECOMOG was perfect because it was made up of soldiers from neighboring countries.

In my fourth year there, we found out about a human crisis unfolding amid the larger crisis. Some 100,000 to 200,000 people were starving in a remote section of Liberia that was generally in the center of the country. They were cut off by the fighting around them, and the only food they had to eat was what they could forage from the jungle.

Most of the suffering were women and children. It was frustrating because at first we could not get there. Neither could ECOMOG's peace-keepers or the United Nations. The people were in a no-man's-land terrorized by rogue rebel forces, most of whom were these crazy young boys armed with automatic weapons they used without compunction or restraint.

Some warlord or other was supposed to be in charge, but it meant nothing in reality. There on the ground, the truth was these dangerous children were under nobody's direct supervision. They really didn't answer to anyone. They had the guns, so for all practical purposes, that made them the boss. When you have guns and you are willing to use them, then you can do anything you want, and they did. That ruthless, anything-goes mentality engendered great fear.

In searching for a solution to the problem, I became aware of a rail line that went right through that central region where the starving people and rebel forces were. The rails went from our warehouses in Buchanan to Yekepa, eighty miles away. The trouble is a train had not been on those tracks for a few years. It was a jungle area and the tracks were all overgrown. There was no way of knowing in advance if the tracks and bridges were intact and if they were rigged with mines.

I needed to secure a train to ride those tracks, and I needed some way to get those rebels to fall in line or back off. There was only one person who held that kind of sway—Charles Taylor. I arranged to speak with him face-to-face in Banga. However, I could not safely drive to Banga as I normally would because of the volatile situation.

In Liberia, August 1993, Father Ken next to a reporter for the *London Times*, and flanked by two members of the West African peacekeeping force, near the train convoy area.

Security concerns required that I look for another method of transportation. I made some inquiries, and a United Nations helicopter was put at my disposal. The pilot flew me and some UN officials into the capital of the Ivory Coast, Yamoussoukro, where we had a small office. A driver took me in a CRS pickup truck to the border town of Danane and from there to Banga. We had to inform peace-keeping forces in real time where we were en route because the road was used to transport black-market weapons, and unauthorized vehicles were prone to attack.

When I finally met with Taylor, I said, "Mr. President"— he loved it when I called him Mr. President—"you know there are more than 100,000 starving people and we can't get there, but the train goes right through the area. Will you give us permission to use that train from Buchanan to Yekepa?"

He could have said no, instead he said, "Go ahead." I returned to Monrovia to set everything up.

The train was powered by a diesel locomotive that normally pulled freight cars loaded with iron ore. The harvesting of iron ore in Yekepa goes back generations. Once the iron ore is mined in Yekepa, it is transported by train to Buchanan and then transferred onto ships. I contacted my manager in Buchanan to apprise him of the arrangement. He put me in touch with the engineer—a guy named Solo Ben. He had studied engineering in the States. He knew what he was doing.

He got the train moving after getting some parts and lubricants brought in from outside the country to make repairs and do maintenance. Officially, there was an embargo on materials coming into Liberia as part of UN-imposed sanctions, which were mainly in place to restrict more arms from ending up in the hands of rebels. But the embargo was porous. The right arrangements could get anything in.

Solo Ben moved the train to Buchanan, where eleven open-air iron-ore freight cars were lined with plastic sheeting and top-loaded with food and medicine. When I left Monrovia to rendezvous with the train in Buchanan, I was turned back by rebel roadblocks. But I had the right contact.

The field marshal from Nigeria named General Olerin who commanded units in ECOMOG was like a brother to me. Anything I needed, all I had to do was contact him, and he would provide me with a gunboat, a military convoy, you name it. He saved the day this time by making available armored ground transport to get me into Buchanan. I joined the train there.

Solo Ben was at the controls, and I was beside him in the engine cabin. We were all set to go when suddenly an ECOMOG general drove up in a jeep to announce, "You're not going anywhere. There are rebels on the tracks, and they're going to stop you and take everything you have."

I was not going to let that stop us, so I conferred with the general and convinced him with, "Let's go, I want to talk to those boys." I will never forget as long as I live the scene that played out next.

We got ourselves inside an ECOMOG tank, and we just plowed right through the jungle. It was raining the whole time. We got to the tracks, and I could see the boys up ahead brandishing their weapons. I told the peace-keepers, "I'm going to go myself," so I walked up the tracks toward that gang of boys. I introduced myself as the director of Catholic Relief Services—everybody knew CRS—and pointed to the CRS T-shirt I wore.

Some of them spoke English. I said, "Do you know there are starving people up the railroad track?"

"Oh yeah, yeah," they responded. "My mother is there…my girlfriend is there." They knew all about it.

I said, "We want to get food to those people, let us through."

The boys said, "Well, we can't make that decision, you'll have to talk to the general."

So they led me into the bush to speak with this rebel general. I asked permission to let the train through and he agreed. But it just didn't feel right, so I had Solo take us back to Buchanan. I suspected the general exerted no real control over the boys, and they would just take everything anyway.

I reached Charles Taylor on the radio. I said, "President Taylor, this is not going to work. I need your strongest general on the train to control the boys along the tracks."

Two nights later there was all this commotion at the arrival of General Coocoo Dennis. He was Taylor's man for smuggling guns into Liberia. He was the meanest, slimiest, baddest guy in the whole world. Everybody was afraid of him. He had a reputation and I knew it. He was the man for the job because we needed to flex some muscle and to do that we had to have someone who was ruthless.

That next morning we got on the train. It was me, Solo Ben, and crazy Coocoo Dennis, with all of his girlfriends along for the ride and his boy soldiers shooting guns in the air from atop a couple of the freight cars in back of the train. It was crazy, it was chaotic.

I had affixed big CRS signs at the front of the engine and on the sides of the train so that people would know this was not Charles Taylor doing this, but CRS. When we got to where the boys were, they let us through without any trouble. The show of force had worked. We started up the tracks to go deeper into the jungle. The train did have to back up many times because the wheels were slipping and spinning on the overgrowth and straining to pull all those iron-ore cars filled to the brim with food and medicine.

We made the trek in one day. Each time we got to an encampment of people, we gave a blast on the horn. These starving souls came out of the bush looking like walking skeletons. We off-loaded food and medicine to them and then went down the line to the next spot where more desperate people were—repeating this scene ten or twelve times.

It was wonderful to bring these people some nourishment and relief. In a number of the places we stopped, the people had not seen a train in years. When they saw it was CRS, more than once they chanted, "C-R-S, C-R-S..." It brought tears to my eyes. I mean, they were literally starving and they were so grateful to receive these supplies.

The effort succeeded beyond my wildest expectations. It was fantastic that all these pieces came together and without interference or disruption. So much could have gone wrong. The train could have broken down or derailed. Coccoo Dennis could have betrayed us. Charles Taylor could have reneged on his promise. One or more of the armed boys could have lost his head. God was with us.

We got to Yekepa that night. I had arranged for my driver to come through Guinea, a neighboring country, to pick me up and take me back to Monrovia, but he could not get through. He was stymied by soldiers. I was stuck in Yekepa while another group of rebels from the north was approaching. I had to find a way to get out of there.

Naturally, I got a hold of Charles Taylor and said, "President Taylor, I need help, I need to get to Buchanan." He told me he had a general in Yekepa named Robinson who could help. I met up with this man—a little pudgy guy—and I caught a ride with him and a few of his soldiers in an old beat-up pickup on a terrible jungle road. There was a problem with one of the tires to boot.

Along the way some armed kids jumped in back and shot their weapons in the air, showing off for their girlfriends. It took us two and a half days. We slept on the ground at night. By the time we reached the outskirts of Buchanan, the general and I were good friends. We were walking shoulder to shoulder into the city when he stopped and said, "Walk behind me." The road was mined, and he knew where the mines were, so we walked like ducks in a row as we approached the city of Buchanan.

We were able to do this relief effort using the train two more times for those starving people. The second time my director of agriculture Ray Studer accompanied the train, and my director of development Krista Riddley went the third time. Neither of those supply runs encountered any problems. And then the war intensified and things became too insecure to continue the effort. I do not know what became of those refugees. It is always the women and children who suffered the most.

As anxious as those adventures were, the most perilous involved a ship, of all things.

We had gotten word that south of Buchanan a mass of people was starving, and the band of rebels in charge there were not letting anyone in or out. I took the unusual measure of leasing a ship, a large freighter by the name of *The Sea Friend*, as a way to bypass the turmoil on the ground. The plan was to load the ship with supplies at the port in Buchanan and go by sea to the port in Greenville near where these people were located.

On my way by jeep to Buchanan, the shelling drew close, which forced me back to Monrovia. After I made a few calls, my field marshal friend General Olerin with ECOMOG put me and some CRS and UN colleagues on a gunship to Buchanan. There, 30,000 metric tons of food were loaded onto this ship's holds.

We sailed all night from Buchanan to Greenville. When we arrived, it was early morning. The procedure was for the ship to turn around and then back into the pier. No ship had been in that pier for years, thus the captain and crew didn't know there was debris down below. As we came along the pier, the ship suffered a serious gash from something in the water, perhaps a metal storage container. We didn't know it for some time. We started off-loading food from the holds unaware anything was wrong and therefore oblivious to the danger.

Liberians lining up to get food supplies (Father Ken standing at the head of the line) from the ship in the port city of Greenville, July 1994. The ship had been damaged and was sinking.

Men and women were lined up to get their rations. At some point we noticed the docked ship was taking on water, though just how badly we didn't know for a couple hours. Then we realized we could not get ourselves out of the area. We ramped up the off-loading.

A general there by the name of Quai Tia, who commanded the rebels in that area, was present with some of his soldiers. He was drunk the whole time. I invited him to come aboard and assist with the off-loading, knowing full well he would abscond with some supplies. But we needed the stuff off the ship because it was becoming clear we were going to lose the vessel.

At one point I was on the pier when I saw a group of armed rebels advancing toward the ship, and I went to them and put my hands out and said, "You're not going to that ship. These supplies are for starving women and children, and you don't look like you're hungry."

Any one of those guys could have shot me and dumped me in the sea right next to where I was standing and that would have been the end of me. But they stopped short of the ship.

General Quai Tia (center) threatened to kill us all as we met on the ship
that was badly damaged and listing in the port city of Greenville,
July 1994. Father Ken (left) and a UN representative handled
negotiations to distribute the food.

As the day drew on, *The Sea Friend* began listing more and more, and we recognized we would have to abandon it soon. Whether we had hours or days, we didn't know. We just knew it was a precarious situation that was only getting worse. Things got more and more chaotic.

At one point Quai Tia accused Fred Gibson, who was with CRS, of selling rice and said he was going to kill him. I said, "You're not going to kill Gibson. He's my man, he's not selling rice."

The general finally backed down. What a spot. Here we were with a sinking ship, frantically trying to get the supplies onto the pier before it was too late, all the while trigger-happy guerillas lurking about and then this madman of a general making threats.

I knew we were going to lose everything—not to the sea, but to the soldiers, whose numbers kept increasing right along with their agitation. The captain's quarters on the ship was the only place to get a call out, and of course they were sending SOS distress messages saying that we needed a rescue helicopter to extract Americans and Europeans.

Contrasted with this life-and-death drama, the captain of the ship had a World Cup football game on the radio between Nigeria and Italy. Finally after three days, a helicopter landed on the pier to evacuate us. Thank God we got out of there with our lives. As I feared would happen, we lost nearly all the supplies to the rebels. Because I arranged to pay per metric ton of food on the ship, CRS did not have to pay for ship repairs.

Liberia was a stark reminder of how little control any of us has over events. Our egos make us believe we can manipulate things to our advantage or desired result. The best we can

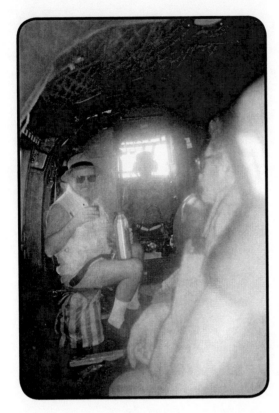

Father Ken took this
photo aboard the rescue
helicopter as the CRS
people were evacuated
from the sinking ship in
Greenville to Monrovia
in Liberia, 1994.
(others unnamed)

hope to do is to affect those things we have a choice in and
then pray that our decisions are in alignment with God's will.
As for other people, they will do what they will do and that
is their own choice. We can only be accountable for our own
individual choice and actions, not theirs.

God's will is not always for us to understand. I do not
think anyone can satisfactorily explain why certain places—
and Liberia is certainly among them—have to face so much
violence year after year, generation after generation, because
of man's inhumanity to man. No one can say why its people
should have to suffer so much when God could, if He chose to
intervene, end it all or mitigate it to a great degree.

So many thousands of Liberians have been oppressed, marginalized, terrorized, murdered, raped, and enslaved. Thousands more have starved and died of disease. After decades of being brutalized by dictators and warlords, Liberia has become a crossroads for terrorists and extremists and every manner of criminal. The flesh-eating disease Ebola has had recent outbreaks there. How much can one people endure? Why should they be singled out for such a cruel string of hardships and tragedies? I do not claim to know.

I do trust, though, that God has a reason for allowing this to go on. I do trust there are lessons in faith to be learned. If nothing else, we should learn by those examples the evil that comes when human life is devalued. All of human life is to be cherished. Each time a life is taken by violence or malice or neglect, all of humanity is injured.

I might have stayed in Liberia but my malaria really kicked in. However, hostilities there might have precluded my being there in the same way I had been before. Stress triggers malaria attacks and despite my mellow nature and iron constitution, the wear and tear of doing humanitarian work in those extreme conditions caught up with me.

The malaria attacks increased in frequency and severity, so much so that I decided I needed to get back to the States. After all those years crossing borders into other countries, I was finally taking the bridge back home. Once back, there would be one more notable excursion outside America before I settled down for good. For all intents and purposes, though, I was coming home, my wayfaring days were over.

14

THE JOURNEY HOME VIA CUBA

O nce I made the decision to return to the States, I knew in my heart I wanted to get back to the Omaha archdiocese and serve again in the inner city, but first I was committed to do fund-raising work for Catholic Relief Services headquarters in Baltimore.

They had asked me to give public talks at colleges and universities and at civic group events all along the East Coast, but mainly in the Baltimore–Washington, DC, area about the good work CRS does and how it depends on donor support to continue this work. Since I am not exactly the shy, retiring type, I welcomed the opportunity. I went out and gave a lot of talks. I enjoyed the experience.

They wanted me to do more speaking, but I said, "No I'm sixty years old, and I want to go back to the archdiocese and work in a parish." I was just really intent on getting back home to Nebraska. I let the archdiocese know of my interest, and in the interim I spent a little more than half a year working in New York City with a sister organization of Catholic Relief Services—the Catholic Medical Mission Board (CMMB). It is ironic that after all that time I spent in developing nations, where people have so little, I should wind up in the center of capitalism, where people are measured by how much they have.

Just like CRS has a proud, long history, CMMB has been doing its "healing and hope" work in countries around the world for more than a century. The faith-based nongovernmental organization focuses on improving health care for the world's poor by building healthy, sustainable communities through community engagement and partnerships. Much of its work focuses on saving the lives of at-risk children and mothers by addressing the leading causes of mortality in Africa, Latin America, and the Caribbean. It collaborates with service providers in host countries to deliver quality health care programs and services without discrimination.

CMMB also distributes food and medicine to crisis areas. During my time with the organization, it maintained a big warehouse in Queens, which served as our main supply depot. When it became evident that vital medicines were in short supply in Cuba, we made preparations to send a big shipment there, but because America had an embargo against Cuba, the plan had to get special approval from the US government.

A Republican on Capitol Hill who opposed the program turned it into a political football, and the controversy around it almost killed the mission before it even started. This

Offloading medicine in Havana.

congressman asserted that Fidel Castro's regime would sell the supplies and keep the money or that at the very least the medicine would never reach its intended recipients, and so he demanded oversight and accountability. And that is how I got tasked with the job of accompanying the shipment, which amounted to $7 million of medicine.

I flew from Miami to Havana, where at the airport I was met by representatives of the Catholic Church there as well as by Cuban government officials. Cuban officials decided what hospitals throughout the island the supplies were going to, and my job was to visit these hospitals to assure Congress and American officials and our donors that the supplies were going to patients and not being diverted and sold on the black market to line someone's pockets.

An airport meeting on the tarmac in Havana. Father Ken in background.

A later meeting with Castro's representatives to arrange to get the medicine to Havana hospitals.

I fully realized that even personally escorting the supplies was no foolproof guarantee they would be properly distributed and dispensed once I left, but that was a risk we were willing to take.

I was in Cuba for a week. Jaime Ortega was the archbishop in Havana then. He is a cardinal now. He was very cooperative. There was no freedom of religion yet at that time in Cuba, but many people were still Catholic. They did not lose their faith, and they realized their faith was really an antidote to a lot of other events taking place around them. I give credit to the priests and the bishops and the archbishop for getting the people to trust in them.

I loved the experience. The Cuban people are easy to like.

It pleases me that during President Barack Obama's last year in office he began the process of the United States normalizing relations with Cuba. I had been an advocate of this happening for the preceding fifty years. It was crazy that we broke off

Meeting with Archbishop Jaime Ortega in Havana (at the head of the table). Father Ken is in the foreground on the right, next to Ken Hackett, the CRS Executive Director.

relations with a neighbor nation with whom we share so much in common. The severing of those ties was done politically to get the Cuban exile vote in Florida. It was all politics.

Obama did exactly the right thing. It should have been done a long time ago by previous administrations. Not only is normalizing relations good for both countries, it is good for the Church. Pope Francis is a good friend of Cardinal Ortega, who has been a strong advocate of renewing relations with the United States. As the press reported, Francis played a key broker's role in bringing American and Cuban officials together to work out the conditions and protocols of reestablishing relations. This is going to strengthen the Church in Cuba and provide more freedom for the people there to practice their faith.

Father Ken was a popular media spokesperson during his brief time in New York. He even had his own radio talk show. Here he is being interviewed for a TV feature.

I left New York for home in 1998 to serve as pastor at St. Lawrence in Silver Creek and St. Peter in Clarks in Nebraska. It was not the inner-city Omaha parish position I requested, but it was a good opportunity because it brought me back to a small-town environment much like the one where I grew up in Clarkson. The assignment gave me a chance to get acclimated to being a parish priest again, which I always say is the best job in town. And it afforded me the chance to get to know the archbishop, Elden Curtiss, who had replaced Daniel Sheehan in my long absence, and for him to understand my love for serving inner-city communities.

I was content to bide my time for two years until a North Omaha post opened up. Sure enough, one did at St. Richard's parish, though the circumstances that brought me there were highly regrettable. After an investigation by law enforcement authorities, the pastor of St. Richard's was convicted of child molestation.

While his case played out, a couple of priests took over at St. Richard's for several months before I arrived, and they and the school principal did a great job shepherding the congregation and the students through a hurtful time. I got the assignment because at that point the archdiocese needed someone there in a permanent capacity who had credibility and experience. The parish was reeling, and the people needed a steady, caring hand to guide them through a process of healing and moving forward.

Those wounds did not heal overnight. I knew going in I would be inheriting a parish still feeling raw and upset by the scandal. Initially my role was to help people deal with the anger and frustration and confusion they felt. Those strong emotions were shared by adults and youths alike.

I did not realize the extent to which it had affected students until one day, months into my pastorship, I walked into a seventh-grade classroom, and the kids started opening up to me. They said, "Father, you know that we love the Church, and the previous pastor disgraced the Church, and we feel very bad about it." They were profoundly affected. We talked it out and discussed how we have to be able to forgive in order to move on.

Healing had to happen with the deposed priest too. I took it upon myself to reach out to him and to try and establish a rapport. We had never met until I visited him at the state penitentiary in Lincoln. Why did I do it? To befriend him. I just thought he needed a friend. He was convicted of doing terrible things, and he was punished by the criminal justice system, by the public scorn focused on him, and by the inner torment of his wrongdoing.

I did not visit him in prison to accuse him or to ask him to make amends. I do not judge people. He was led into the room where prisoners receive visitors, and I said, "Can't we be friends? Can't we communicate?" and he turned around and walked away. I went back a second time. This time he stayed and we talked.

By the time I got to St. Richard's, the congregation was almost all white and the school was almost all black, which reflected a pattern that played out in many other inner-city Catholic parishes and schools. There are few black Catholics to begin with, and in a city like Omaha, the vast majority of them have attended St. Benedict the Moor. Even though St. Richard's was near a black neighborhood, its congregation always had been predominantly white. For a long time the school served mostly white students whose parents were parish members and who in many cases had graduated from the school themselves. But over time, more and more parishioners moved out of the neighborhood and sent their children to other schools. It is hard to establish community when people are not living in the parish and they don't understand the area.

At the same time, the congregation grew older, with fewer and fewer members having school-age children. Increasingly, the school served African-American youth from the neighborhood, almost all of whom were non-Catholic.

Another phenomenon that my arrival coincided with was the emergence of a large South Sudanese refugee population in Omaha. Many Sudanese are Catholic. I intentionally developed a rapport with the local Sudanese community and that resulted in having many of their children in our school and more and more Sudanese families at our worship services. Even though my experiences in Africa were on the west coast of that vast continent, and I never visited the eastern region, where Sudan is located, these encounters in America with Sudanese refugees were strong reminders of my time in Africa.

The net exodus of parishioners, though, continued and the parish began to decline. The school still served a number of children and people still supported the church. We worked damn hard at remaining relevant and keeping things going.

The year I left, we were still able to pay our bills. St. Richard's was providing stability to people in that area. But the writing was on the wall because other inner-city parishes were serving the same niche, and there were only so many students and families to go around. Eventually the school was closed. The same thing has happened to several other Catholic schools and churches in Omaha's older neighborhoods, where the population to feed many different Catholic parishes and schools just isn't there anymore. As closings occur, congregations and enrollments become consolidated at one site. The same thing has been happening in cities across America.

During my tenure at St. Richard's, I also tended to another inner-city parish, St. Therese of the Child Jesus, an even smaller community of worshipers. It too has since been closed. It is sad when a parish closes, but at least the former St. Richard's is being put to good use in the form of an intergenerational campus that has opened there. The campus includes residential housing for young families and seniors as well as an array of health and other services. The nearby Blessed Sacrament parish closed only a few years after St. Richard's, and blessedly it too is being repurposed for a positive new use, in this case as a free school for inner-city youth.

All in all I enjoyed my time at St. Richard's very much. We made the best of some bad circumstances and some radical changes all impinging on the parish at the same time. I enjoyed working with the school and the kids and the adults.

While there, I got involved with a new social action organization, Omaha Together One Community (OTOC), that brought together different faith-based groups to address some of Omaha's long-festering problems. Through house meetings and community canvassing, we identified issues such as poverty, inequitable housing, police abuse, the need for an independent police auditor, and pay disparities, and we devised strategies to advocate for positive change with stakeholders and elected leaders.

As new minority populations began appearing in numbers, including Latinos and Sudanese, we recognized bridges needed building between these communities and the majority community. When meat-packing workers attempting to organize a union in order to negotiate safer working conditions met resistance from employers, we advocated on the workers' behalf. Most of these workers were Hispanic immigrants, many of them undocumented, and a fair number were from Africa.

This social-conscious work was right up my alley and reminded me a bit of those heady times in the 1960s when social change was in the air and I was on the front lines of efforts to oppose injustice and achieve equity.

My work with OTOC and other social justice causes put me in regular contact with a fellow man of faith whom I greatly admire, Rabbi Aryeh Azriel. He is the longtime leader of Omaha's reform synagogue, Temple Israel, which has a rich history. Rabbi Azriel, a native of Israel, has been an interfaith champion for many years, purposefully reaching out to other faith groups, Christians and Muslims alike, through events and activities that promote harmony.

Immediately in the wake of the 9/11 attacks, he organized a cordon of Jews and Christians to protect a local mosque from any attempted harm. He is a driving force behind the Tri-Faith Initiative in Omaha that seeks to create an interfaith campus with Jewish, Muslim, and Christian houses of worship and a shared communal space. He led his congregation to relocate to the site for the campus. In 2013 Temple Israel moved into the new synagogue it built there. His work in this regard is a true inspiration.

On a personal note, he has served as my close friend for several years now. My trust and respect for him is such I have asked him to say my eulogy at my funeral, and he has kindly agreed to do so.

It was not just working with the Sudanese or Hispanic communities that brought me back to my experiences overseas, it was that darn malaria I originally contracted in Yemen. From that point forward, malaria has been an unwelcome companion wherever I have gone.

I remember I detected I was having a particularly bad malaria attack when I was at St. Richard's. It was a Sunday morning. I had an eight o'clock Mass, and as I was walking across the parking lot to the church, I noticed this telltale bunching up of the nerves and I said to myself, "My God, I'm coming down with malaria."

I got through that service, but then I had an eleven o'clock Mass. I didn't have any medicine of my own because I had not had an attack in a good long while. It occurred to me there were a lot of Africans in the congregation. So before that second Mass, I asked the Sudanese in the pews, "Do any of you have any malaria medicines?" and sure enough this lady did and she gave me some.

I didn't take the meds right away though. Without meds I made it through the second service but just barely, as by the end I was beginning to shake and sweat and get feverish. When Mass was over, I made my way back to the rectory, took the medication, and laid down, thinking the symptoms would subside. But in no time at all, I was almost shaking out of the bed, the trembling was so bad. I decided I could not tough this one out, so I took myself to Creighton Medical Center. Good thing, too, because I was so sick that time that I ended up staying there three days with an intravenous feed.

For stretches of time I can almost forget I have malaria until it rears its ugly head again. Or I can make myself believe I am over and done with it until something happens to remind me. For example, a few years ago I had my annual physical and I said to my doctor, "Thank God, I don't have malaria anymore."

But he said, "Get this straight, Ken, you *do* have malaria. Once you have it, there's no getting rid of it. It doesn't just go away." But he confirmed that the reason the attacks have subsided since that bad one that put me in the hospital when I was at St. Richard's is that my body is finally able to cope with the malaria after all these years. The bug inside me has been rendered inactive. It works the same with leprosy.

You never really get some places out of your system and that is true of St. Richard's. To this day I retain close relationships with several folks who were parishioners there. A couple dozen of us get together once a month for lunch. We go to a northwest Omaha buffet for what has become our Brunch Bunch. It is an enjoyable way to stay connected with people I care about and who care about me. One of the benefits of being a pastor is that the parish adopts you as one of their own, and the people there become like a family to you.

Though my experience at St. Richard's proved quite positive, and it enriched my life with new friends, when I was reassigned to St. Benedict the Moor, I was delighted. The truth is that once I came home to the States to stay and let the Omaha archdiocese know of my desire to serve the inner city, my eyes were on St. Benedict's all along. It took a few stops and several years before I eventually got there, but it was well worth the wait.

My four years at St. Ben's were among the best years of my life. It is a small but fiercely dedicated black congregation. It is my fervent desire and prayer that St. Benedict's never close. It is unlikely to happen in the foreseeable future because it still serves as the hope for black Catholics in Omaha. Unless and until its base of membership moves away or stops coming, it should remain a viable bastion and anchor for that community. Any premature attempt at closing it would raise such ire that I think the archdiocese would have to reconsider.

I insisted right off that I live in the rectory next to the church. The parish had been without a regular priest for a year and a half, and no priest had lived in that rectory for more than a decade. The residence needed a good going over because the parish had let a family displaced from Hurricane Katrina live there for a time, and they tore the whole place up. It was a real shambles.

Before I came on the scene, the pastors serving the Church were always Jesuits, and instead of living in the rectory, they lived at the clergy center at the nearby Jesuit university, Creighton. But that arrangement created a certain disconnect between the priests who had Mass and presided over baptisms, weddings, and funerals at the church and the people who worshiped there and lived in the neighborhood. You have got to live there if you are truly going to be a part of people's lives.

I became the first non-Jesuit to pastor there. Now, just to be clear, I officially served as the associate pastor under a Jesuit who had the title of pastor. But the truth of the matter is he was never there, so in all actuality I was the pastor serving the people on a day-to-day basis. And right from the start I loved it there. I still do.

All my previous experience in the inner city well prepared me for the assignment. It helped me to understand African-Americans a little bit better. My experiences around the world also gave me a perspective in being able to accept people where they are. By the time I came to St. Ben's, I was a more mature and seasoned priest. The skill sets to run giant aid programs in Africa or Asia are not necessarily applicable to running an inner-city parish or school in the United States. But just the same, I was able to bring to bear certain expertise from one setting to the other. I learned new things in the bargain. I loved it. I also had the advantage of going to St. Ben's directly after spending all those years at a similar inner-city parish, St. Richard's, which proved a good transition for me.

Of course, the big difference between St. Richard's and St. Ben's is that while the former was a white parish in a black neighborhood, the latter was and is a black parish in a black neighborhood. African-Americans are by and large very loving, warm people, and the people of St. Ben's opened their hearts to me and I in turn opened mine to them. We developed a deep feeling for each other.

No matter what parish you go to, you need to understand its history, you need to study it in order to appreciate what makes it unique. In the case of St. Benedict's, I learned just what a valued refuge and sanctuary it had been for blacks in an era when people of color were not warmly received at mainstream Catholic white parishes. Blacks were outsiders practically everywhere else in the Catholic Church, but this one place was their very own haven for expressing their faith. It was in their neighborhood too. It was not the white man's church. It was their church, one where they could be themselves and bring aspects of their culture to the art on the walls, to the liturgy, to the food, and to other traditions.

The people of St. Benedict's formed a strong, close identity with each other as folks sharing the same race, the same culture, the same faith, and the same hard road to equality.

NOT FINISHED YET

M y curiosity about the world remains strong. I am every bit as engaged in social justice issues as before. When I see wrong, I feel compelled to make things right, if only by raising my voice or lifting my pen to be heard. I have lost none of my vim and vigor when it comes to confronting oppression. My progressive humanist views that some label as ultra liberal have not softened or weakened with age or time. Quite the opposite has occurred. I continue to challenge authority figures when their power isolates them from the will of the people.

One thing I have learned in my many travels is that people are fundamentally the same everywhere, from Clarkson to Calcutta. But not everyone has the same advantages as others do. Much of my work as a priest has been with disadvantaged, disenfranchised populations. I realized I could not make a lasting difference in people's lives sitting behind a desk. I had to go to them. I walked in their shoes and lived among them. Crossing many bridges to do so.

When I was a young priest in the 1960s, the Church was immersed in social justice. These were the years of Martin Luther King Jr., John Kennedy, and Bobby Kennedy. The activist church of that era sent priests out into the black and Chicano communities to get a grassroots understanding of what the issues were. We were making progress. We could see that discrimination was being addressed.

But then the Church retreated into conservatism and isolationism for the next four or five decades. Now Pope Francis is turning this around and calling on priests, who had grown distant from the fray, to get involved again by rolling up their sleeves and working with the people as they find them on the ground. He is urging priests to get out of the pulpit and to engage the poorest of the poor. It is what being a pastor is all about.

Francis released a mission statement for his papacy that says the Catholic Church and the papacy itself must be reformed to create a more missionary and merciful church that gets its hands dirty as it seeks out the poor and oppressed.

> Reinvigorate the Church's evangelical zeal in a world marked by indifference, secularization, and vast income inequalities. More than by fear of going astray, my hope is that we will be moved by the fear of remaining shut up within structures which give us a false sense of security, within rules which make us harsh judges, within habits which make us feel safe, while at our door

people are starving and Jesus does not tire of
saying to us, "Give them something to eat."

Pope Francis says the Church's greatest concern must be
the poor and marginalized, "since they are victims of an unjust,
global economic system that prizes profit over people—the
poor need the tender, merciful love the Church can provide."
He challenges the world's priests to bring the healing
power of God's grace to everyone in need, to stay close to the
marginalized, and to be "shepherds living with the smell of the
sheep." When a priest "doesn't put his own skin and own heart
on the line, he never hears a warm, heartfelt word of thanks"
from those he has helped, the pope says.

Simply put, we are called to be fishers of men. To heed
that call requires going where the people are. I can speak from
experience that crossing bridges to engage people has taught
me humility and gratitude. The willingness to go outside my
comfort zone has exposed me to a much wider arena of life.
It is true, I have seen much suffering. Yet even in the midst of
unimaginable poverty and hunger, I have seen great beauty. I
have witnessed people share a few precious grains of rice with
their neighbors. My greatest teachers have been the poor and
the ostracized. They have some of the most beautiful, caring
souls. Despite their hardship, many choose to live joyfully and
gratefully—a lesson for us all.

I was asked once, "After all the suffering you saw, is your
faith stronger or weaker?" I don't know the answer to that. The
places where I worked overseas—Yemen, India, Bangladesh,
Nepal, Liberia—were such different situations than any I
encountered in the States, but boy they were a great gift for me.

I know I was blessed to have had those firsthand experiences to work directly with the neediest and the poorest of the poor, and to be able to administer programs that could lift these people up and empower them. Not many people get the opportunity to experience what I did.

Whoever you are and no matter what you do, you will come upon bridges of one sort or another at various points in your life. The decision to cross or not to cross is yours. What you do when you arrive on the other side is up to you.

The very first bridge I crossed was choosing to study for the priesthood, a decision that took me and everyone who knew me by surprise. Then came a series of bridges that once crossed brought me into contact with diverse peoples and their incredibly different yet similar needs.

So, you see, I am still a simple man at heart. It has served me well all these years wherever I have made my bed—in a crowded Yemeni jail after my arrest while serving God in a leper village, or sleeping on a dirt floor hardened with cow dung in a hut. If this simple old priest has learned anything, it is the truth of the old saying, "Home is where the heart is." I have truly felt at home in all my wanderings. And unlike that other old saying, "You can't go home again," I have found that I can.

I am content being rooted back in my homeland, but my thoughts of those distant other homes I had the privilege of serving are never far from my thoughts and prayers.

To be unimportant and to humbly do things that nobody would know about has been my sincere desire, which is one of the reasons I did not want to write this book. It is sure to bring attention to me that perhaps I should not have sought. And so I pray this account of my life is not a personal spectacle but a recounting of a most wonderful journey serving God. May its discoveries and experiences inspire your own life story of service.

FINAL CROSSING

◆

As I am apt to say, I have never met a stranger. Everyone I meet is my friend. That is not to imply I always like what people do or that I always agree or get along with everyone. Personalities and values may clash, but that does not mean we cannot be friends, at least in spirit. Besides, who am I to judge? I am certainly not without fault or sin; therefore, I am in no position to cast stones.

The human race is like a giant family, and as in any family, there are bound to be disputes and differences. That comes with the territory. All my journeys have proven to me the simple but profound truth that we human beings—regardless of our race or nationality or political-religious beliefs—all want the same basic things. We want to be loved, we want to be free, we want our lives to have meaning and purpose, and we want to be respected.

Everywhere I have gone, even when I did not speak the language and did not know the customs, I have managed to fit in because I have been intentional about meeting people where they are and acknowledging them as individuals who are loved by God. I also made a sincere effort to learn the language and the lifestyle.

When we put labels on people and try to box them into some category, we diminish them because then they become less fully human in our eyes. Once we discard stereotypes, we see people for who they truly are and not for some figment of our imagination or for some convenient assumption. My outspoken advocacy for human rights issues has gotten me into hot water.

God has gifted me with the ability to look past differences and to see people's hearts. When you are an extrovert and a lover, life is great, and I assure you that I am both an extrovert and a lover. Therefore, life is wonderful in my eyes.

The values I learned growing up—to be fair, to be honest, to love people—have served me well as a priest. I learned from my family to have a heart for social justice. I learned to accept people in a loving way. I learned not to judge someone merely by the color of their skin. There was no racism in our family. We looked upon people of color very positively. I was taught everybody is the same, everybody is equal. I had a wonderful background that way.

If I had not come from such a loving background, my growing up might have ill-prepared me for the heterogeneous world we live in and that I came to experience firsthand once I left my parochial youth behind. That is because there was little diversity in the small, rural Czech community of Clarkson, Nebraska, where I came of age.

I have tried to make clear by my words and actions that I do not take stances that offend the Church just to stir the pot or to be a fly in the ointment. Rather, I speak the truth as I see it, and I pray that by what I advocate, my dissident voice be added to the multitude of voices calling for change. When leadership, whether secular or religious, becomes disconnected from the people, bad things happen or, even worse, nothing changes. Expressing opposing views, asking tough questions, taking unpopular or disapproved-of stands, and offering constructive criticism all help to keep leadership accountable and responsive to changing conditions and attitudes.

As I write these words, I am heartened by the increasingly strong stance Pope Francis is taking in moving the Church to include gays and lesbians and divorced Catholics in its unequivocal embrace. At the 2014 synod of bishops, he actually had explicit language welcoming these populations in the drafts of the synod document. Even though the final document excluded that language, he has now emphatically signaled the Church is moving in the direction of inclusion, perhaps faster than many bishops would like. But make no mistake about it, the pope is leading this movement, and the Church's hierarchy, reluctant or not, will follow.

Having entered the eighth decade of life and having put down on paper this considered reflection of that life, I am filled with gratitude for all the persons and experiences God has put along my path. I am grateful for all the bridges I have had the opportunity to cross. I have learned so much in the process of making these journeys, both literal and figurative.

My eyes have opened to new cultures, new ways of living, new modes of being. My heart has grown full from all the kindnesses shown me. My soul has been enriched by the human suffering and goodness I have witnessed. My mind has been expanded by the scale of this world and by the abundance of good and inexorable evil bound up in it.

Cross with me, my brothers and sisters, into the rapture of living. Not everything will be pleasant. Not everything you want or need will be immediately forthcoming. Nothing is guaranteed us. It is impossible to avoid pain and discomfort, disappointment and failure. You will stumble and fall and make mistakes. There will be wrong turns and false starts. But to everything there is a season. And if we only put our trust in God and surrender to His will, things will work out according to His plan, and you will doubtless find prosperity and serenity if that is what you seek.

In recalling the events of my life for this book, particularly those experiences overseas, I asked myself, *Did I really do those things? Did I really live in a dirt-floor hut and work with lepers for five years in Yemen? Did I really work fourteen years for Catholic Relief Services in India, Bangladesh, Nepal, and Liberia?* Yes, my friends, I really did, though sometimes it does not even seem real to me. More like a dream. But I have the pictures, passport, visa, and reports to prove it. The malaria too. Praise God for opportunities I was given to serve people in such different lands.

It is my prayer that the travels and experiences I describe in these pages serve as guideposts to help you navigate your own wanderings and crossings.

A bridge of some sort is always before you. It may lead to a place, to a culture, to a job, to a mission, to an opportunity, to a new start, to a new lifestyle, to new relationships, to new insights, to any number of things. On your journey, never be afraid to open your heart and speak your mind. We are all called to be witnesses. We are all called to testify. To make the crossing, all that is required is a willing and trusting spirit. Go ahead, make your way over to the other side. God is with you every step of the way. Take His hand and follow. Many riches await.

As a lifelong bridge-crosser, I can attest to these truths. Go and grow. Go in peace. May your journey give you the expanded vision and joy my journeys have given me.

---◆---

All proceeds from this
book will be donated to:

Catholic Relief Services
The Archdiocese of Omaha
Catholic Charities

Thank you!

---◆---